CH00539328

Clothing the Play

The Art and Craft of Stage Design

Clothing the Play

The Art and Craft of Stage Design

by Roswitha Spence

AWSNA

Printed with support from the Waldorf Curriculum Fund

Published by:
The Association of Waldorf Schools
of North America
Publications Office
38 Main Street
Chatham, NY 12037

Title: *Clothing the Play*
        The Art and Craft of Stage Design
Author: Roswitha Spence
Editor: David Mitchell
Copyeditor, Proofreader, Layout: Ann Erwin
Manuscript Preparation: Sarah Kane
Illustrations, Designs and Costumes: Roswitha Spence
Photographs: Charlotte Fischer

© 2012 by AWSNA
ISBN # 978-1-936367-25-2

Printed in China

Contents

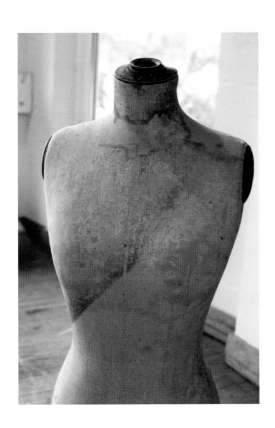

Preface: Dawn Langman

Introduction: Roswitha Spence

Chapter I: An Approach to Design

Chapter II: Color

Chapter III: Textures

Chapter IV: Style & Form

Chapter V: Costume

Chapter VI: Makeup, Mask & Puppetry

Chapter VII: Scenery

Chapter VIII: Lighting

Chapter IX: Application & Examples

Chapter X: *Pericles, Prince of Tyre*

Chapter XI: Exercises

Chapter XII: Practical Issues

Index of Characters

Bibliography

Acknowledgements

Preface

For ten years I was privileged to work beside Roswitha on the annual production of a Shakespeare play. This took place at Emerson College in Sussex, England. Together we would attempt to penetrate the deeper levels of each play. Then we would separate: she to her team of students who would learn with her how to clothe the play and myself to the group who would ultimately wear the costumes and inhabit those spaces that she has written of in the following pages.

At various times during the weeks leading to the performances, both groups would meet and share the results of their journeys. Invariably Roswitha would inspire the entire group with the profound truths of what her team was creating visually. It was always a wonder for me to see that what I was striving for in the creation of the characters and the interactions by the actors could be embodied in color and style. Again and again I was astonished at Roswitha's unique combination of practical and professional expertise infused with spiritual insight.

This penetration of the elements of color and style in clothing and setting aroused an atmosphere of sacred wonder in the actors and a profound respect for the role of those who worked behind the scenes. She showed how these elements emerged out of the lawfulness which underlies the whole evolving creation of both our human world and the world of nature.

I was granted a rare glimpse of something not experienced since. Very often the various components of a production arise arbitrarily out of each separate department. However, this has been a working together which enabled all the aspects to serve the greater whole. This may be expressed as the spiritual core of the play or the central intention within the playwright's inspiration.

Over the years I have witnessed Roswitha's incredible range of talents, of which only a few are represented in this book. In all she attempts she achieves a quality of excellence. There is a devotion to detail, not in a pedantic way but out of an understanding of how all the parts, even the tiniest, spring from the central creative vision that informs the whole. Together with her willingness to master the discipline that each medium requires, she has achieved that capacity of the true artist: to render the medium transparent so that it can reveal the deeper levels of reality that lie behind surface appearances. She has achieved this mastery in a number of realms, some of which are considered to be technical only. In this she has demonstrated that a craft becomes an art when the technical skills serve the creative impulse of the soul, and that a discipline is not simply the practice of cold, empty form but devoted practice to master the creative laws of the universe. Like all those who achieve mastery, she can play and find creative solutions even when working with the minimum of resources.

This book is filled with practical treasures and is welcomed by all of us who have for many years acknowledged the unique work Roswitha has developed. It will be valued by everyone who longs to have guidance at a practical level which is also inspired by a deeper vision.

Dawn Langman
Melbourne, Australia

Introduction

"All the world's a stage,
And all the men and women merely players;..."
As You Like It, Act II, scene 7

In the photograph a little girl is sitting in her cot beside a teddy bear almost as large as herself. As she gazes intently at the camera, she sucks the thread she is about to push through the eye of a needle: Three-year-old Roswitha is making her first costume, an elaborate Elizabethan affair in deep red velvet with a gold trim, for her favorite doll. It is a glorious mess, but she is thrilled with the result!

As a professional eurythmist or movement artist, my mother wore pure silk costumes on stage in vibrant shades of many colors that often hung around the walls of our flat. I remember them as always being freshly ironed. I would revel in diving in and out among them and letting the fabrics slide through my fingers. Looking back, it is remarkable that my mother never told me not to. My father taught history of art and wood-carving and spent many hours after school working on some project or other that nearly always included my brother Christopher and me. I had the good fortune to have had parents who taught me from an early age that almost everything can be created at home and made both beautiful and practical. I also learned that compromise, either in practicality or in beauty, is not an option.

When I started school, I discovered the joy of all arts and crafts, and I would be first in line to help with costumes for the many plays we performed. So it was no surprise to my parents and teachers that, on leaving school, I chose to train in designing and making theatre costumes. Once I finished my training, for which I had gone to Stuttgart, Germany, I started work as a cutter at The English National Opera in the production wardrobe, and later I spent a season working for The Royal Shakespeare Company in Stratford-upon-Avon. In between I was employed in a modern couture house, where I made an important discovery about the difference between stage costume and street clothes: Everyday wear, especially when custom-made, needs to be perfect on the inside and even neater than on the outside, so that the individual wearing the garment feels comfortable and 'at home' in it. This is not true of the stage costume, the outside of which is more important than the inside, and whilst both outside and inside must be secure and comfortable, neither needs to be as neatly finished as streetwear.

Later, life took me to Emerson College in Sussex, England, an adult education and training center based on the work of Rudolf Steiner and anthroposophy. Though not part of the daily or weekly timetable, drama was taken up enthusiastically and actively by the students. In the winter there were performances of Christmas plays adapted from the English mediaeval mystery cycles and in the summer productions of Shakespeare's works. The founder, Francis Edmunds, had a great love of Shakespeare and awoke in me a new understanding of his plays that strengthened my own love of them, as year after year we studied the plays and rehearsed the productions that the students then performed.

I found it immensely exciting to search for depths of meaning within the images within the text, only to discover how anthroposophy could awaken quite new levels of understanding of the plays. I learned first how both earthly and spiritual truths can be found in the texts, and then how the use of **color** can make these truths accessible to the audience, how the **textures** of cloth and painted surfaces can translate the color into movement and how the **style** and shape of any piece of scenery or garment objectively sets the timeframe for the story the play tells. When the designing process uses these principles in this sequence, it creates cohesion between the spoken word and the visual appearance of the play.

During my years in professional theatre, I worked with the sketches given by the stage designers. They were nearly always exceptional works of art, drawn and painted with skill. The costume style was, in the main, true to history, and

attached to one corner of each sketch were swatches or small samples of the fabrics chosen for each part of the garment. When the sketches entered our workshop, they were accompanied by the great bolts of the fabrics that had just been bought for the costumes. In this moment the designer's creative process was complete, except for the costume fittings, while my own, the interpretation and execution of the costumes, was just beginning.

However, I found I could not use this way of working when I began to teach students, and so I started to develop another way that would incorporate all three areas of theatre design. Set, lighting and costume are conventionally designed by three different people, and the three main ingredients—color, texture and style—work differently in the three areas. But because I was responsible for the overall design, I had the opportunity to incorporate every aspect of the three ingredients into the three areas and to discover how they relate to and affect each other.

A moment of intuition led me to start the designing process with color. Whenever I started to live with the inner substance of a play, in my mind's eye I saw moving swaths of varying color tones. It was as if I was gathering these colors from vast, unseen spaces, drawing the many individual strands together and gradually weaving them into a whole within myself. I then added the texture to the colors and formed them into a style. When I saw on stage the results of this approach to design, I was astonished to discover how

10

Top: School days   *Bottom: College days*

different the effect could be from what I had learned in training. When the starting point of the process was the style or form, I sensed that the colors were held or contained within each character, but when color was the starting point, they seemed to move and flow between the characters and enrich the wholeness of the production.

When I began to teach backstage art and craft, I started by using my ready-made sketches, but my students were not prepared to work with ideas on paper that they had not participated in developing. And so I began to evolve exercises in which the students themselves researched the elements that belong to the designing of a theatre production. Many who joined the backstage team had not learned any arts or crafts when growing up, so our productions led them to discover how creative their minds and hearts and how skillful their hands could be. It also became important to balance artistic work with the crafting activities that were needed to dress or clothe both stage and actors. I witnessed with great pleasure how many of the students discovered the following: Without artistry the craftsmanship is dull, just as without manual abilities the artistic cannot shine.

The approach I have developed and that I have set out in this book can be applied to any stage production. Wherever there are actors, in whatever setting, whatever their appearance and in whatever light, the visual aspect affects any audience. For the sake of clarity, however, I have chosen to focus on Shakespeare's plays, as those are the ones I have designed most frequently.

Over the years, colleagues and students have asked me to write about this approach, and now that this has become reality, perhaps the contents of this book will help those whose task it is to clothe a play and who might not know where to begin, or inspire those who wish to find a new approach to their profession of stage design. First and foremost, it intends not to give answers, but to generate new questions, support and strengthen individual initiative and, above all, encourage free creativity. In whatever the circumstances individuals may find themselves working with color, texture and style in set, costume and lighting, I hope that the following chapters will prove useful to all with an interest in *Clothing the Play*.

Roswitha Spence
Emerson College, 2012

I

AN APPROACH TO DESIGN

"... the play's the thing,

Wherein I'll catch the conscience of the king."

Hamlet, Act II, scene 2

I once attended a performance of a production in which one scene was set in a kitchen. The overall setting was bland, with off-white wallpaper, windows with peeling, colorless paint, faded curtains and a floor covered in dull, worn linoleum. At the center of the stage stood a battered table and chair. An elderly couple entered, the wife dressed in a shabby cover-all apron and the husband in baggy trousers held up with suspenders over a collarless shirt. Their conversation was a habitual argument that had long lost its heat. During this dialogue the husband cautiously climbed onto the rickety chair and then onto the table to change the naked light bulb. Taking what seemed like an eternity to do so, this old man, with bent back and arthritic knees, held the audience spellbound. This was the artistic genius of Lawrence Olivier at work, giving deep significance to the most mundane of activities.

FIRST GOALS

There are three elements that a designer may want to bear in mind when approaching the design of a play and searching for the specific focus of the production: telling the story, engaging the audience and supporting the actors.

Telling the Story: Two points are worth remembering in relation to the story of a play: However beautiful the visual aspect of a production may be, it frames and supports the story and therefore should not compete for the audience's attention, and it rests with the designer to create both images and practical solutions that do this. At the same time the designer's aim is to open the audience's eyes to a dimension beyond what is said in the script, that heightens the audience's understanding of the story and

enhances the writer's and director's intentions. So the designer needs to reflect on how to bring out certain aspects of the story with visual tools, not only when first imagining and sketching it, but also when developing the design further during rehearsals, when the stage and the actors have become physical realities.

Engaging the Audience: Precisely because it happens unconsciously, everything to do with the visual side of a production influences the audience's experience profoundly, and the overall relationship between color, texture and style—and between costume, set and lighting—can either diminish or enhance it. So the set, costume and lighting design can give the audience the impression that they are participating in the action themselves or that they are entirely outside it. Therefore, another goal of the designer might be to create a design that allows

the audience to engage actively with what happens on stage. It is also worth remembering that the production is complete only when the production has an audience, and the performers can engage in an inner dialogue with those watching. This silent encounter may take both actor and spectator beyond the worlds they know and lift the design, as part of the whole production, into a dimension that is filled with life.

Supporting the Actors: Thirdly, actors need colors, textures and styles in set, costume and lighting that encourage them to enter their roles and to engage the full scope of their talents. They also need to know that their surroundings are safe and their costumes comfortable so that they can move around with ease and confidence.

DEVELOPING
THE OVERALL VISION

In an ideal world the first step for the designer is to meet the director and other members of the creative team to work on an approach to or vision of the play. It is also helpful—this is particularly valuable when designing for an amateur production—to get to know the company in some depth, and when the company of actors and the backstage crew are included in this exploration of the play from the start, a valuable cohesion can be established. The aim is to explore what the play has to offer and to discover how each individual can bring his or her own insights to enrich the overall vision. If the company members have been encouraged to become co-creators from the outset, the designer can specifically ask actors for their input regarding the colors and moods of the play and its characters.

This exploration and discussion will allow the creative team to discover the many choices that it needs to make as quickly as possible. These choices obviously present challenges, but they are also opportunities: Which aspect of the play's story does the company want to tell? How deeply do those involved wish to penetrate the play? What 'world' do they choose to portray?

Then there are practicalities that strongly influence the first work of the designer: Will the production be realistic or stylized? Will the play be set indoors or outdoors or both? Is the space to be used for the production a conventional stage with a proscenium arch? Does the stage have a thrust, or does it offer the opportunity to perform in the round? Will the production perform in one venue only or tour? What is the overall production budget?

Questions asking for early artistic resolutions have in my experience of working on a Shakespeare play included the following: *Twelfth Night* is usually considered to be pure comedy; can it also be tragic, if the laughter it raises is frequently cruel and isolates the victims? *King Lear* is generally classified as a tragedy; is it a tragedy if the main character goes mad but at the end overcomes his madness and becomes truly wise? In *Pericles* the hero goes on an epic voyage; is it an outer event, an inner journey or both at the same time?

RESEARCHING

1. READING & IMAGINING

My starting point is to clear my mind of previous designs and, with a 'blank canvas' in my imagination as well as an attitude of waiting or listening for images, to study the play. I read it repeatedly, often twelve to fifteen times, in different ways and with different goals, for example, the whole play in one session, to acquire an overview; one act slowly, each day, to deepen my understanding of it; characters only, one at a time, to experience their individual qualities, their perspective and development. In this way I can identify with the overall journey of the play from every angle. Out of these readings my first images arise.

2. OBSERVING

Such images have led me to observe and explore particular places and to study related material. For example, when preparing for a production of *Pericles*, a story of ocean voyages, I went to the south English coast. Watching how the water moved, I imagined Pericles spending many hours riding that movement on his ship. I noticed that the random rolling of the pebbles against each other contrasted with the rhythmical ebb and flow of the water, but was similar to the seemingly random ways in which Pericles arrived at the various countries he visits. Then I saw how the sun on the moving ripples created patches of intense light and shadow in everchanging shapes, and I saw them as a metaphor for the joys and woes that Pericles experiences. The three different qualities of movement in water, stone and light gave me the key to understanding the varying situations and moods of the play as well as the tools for its design.

3. LIVING INTO THE SCRIPT

A script is like the street map of an unknown city about to be explored; it needs to be closely studied so that the designer can live within it comfortably. A good place to start the exploration is with what the designer meets first: the title. *A Midsummer Night's Dream,* for example, describes the season and the time of day, as well as the dreamy nature of the characters' awareness. In his first lines Theseus, Duke of Athens, specifies the season and time:

"... four happy days bring in
Another moon; but O! methinks how slow
This old moon wanes; ..."
and the words convey that the play opens on one of the darkest nights of high summer. Puck's closing words then reconnect with the final word in the title and invite the audience to acknowledge that just as the characters have been dreaming so, too, have they:
"...That you have but slumber'd here
While these visions did appear..."

When designing this play I used the title to create the main image and then gave the entire set the visual quality of an archetypal dream. Its edges were blurred, and at the center I placed what I called a 'window' of focus. This translated into flats at the borders of the space painted midnight-blue and basic costumes in dark fabrics that were later covered with garments lighter in tone and texture.

Shakespeare's **character names** are often revealing. Celia's name in *As You Like It* contains within it the Latin word for heaven, *coelus*, and dressing her in a heavenly or celestial blue can heighten this aspect of her character. The name of her cousin, Rosalind, comes from the Latin word *rosa*, and although these flowers can have many colors, the classic one is red, and dressing Rosalind in red can emphasize what Shakespeare may have wanted to convey with her name. Then, blue and red are clearly contrasting colors and can help the actors find the contrasts in their characters.

Developing this perspective further, these two colors live side by side in mediaeval paintings of Mary, the Madonna, by such artists as Raphael. The red of Mary's dress expresses the warmth and love within her heart for her child; the heavenly blue of the cloak surrounds the dress and can be understood as the expression of Mary's openness to the infinite wisdom of God. The tones of the red and blue chosen for Rosalind and Celia can echo what is contained within this image.

Celia, *As You Like It*: "When I was helped into this costume, I was concerned because the underskirt is tremendously heavy and the waist and jacket snug. But a surprising thing happened once I had it on: When I started running around and giggling with Lara, it ceased to be uncomfortable and I forgot I was wearing a costume. Despite its weight I remember feeling compelled to move more than in any of the other costumes I had tried on." - Brigitte*

Rosalind, *As You Like It*: "The heavy, layered underskirt made my movement feel grounded. The way the skirt pulled me in at the waist gave me a helpless, feminine feeling that was in contrast to the earthy skirting." - Lara

There are of course countless secrets to be found in **individual words and phrases**. The following were ones that spoke to me when I was preparing the design for a production of *The Winter's Tale*. In the belief that his queen, Hermione, has been unfaithful with his closest friend, Leontes, king of Sicilia, expresses his inner turmoil in the following way:
"I have tremor cordis on me."
In experiencing her husband's deep hurt and anger, Hermione senses the darkness of the external forces controlling him:
"There's some ill planet reigns."

Although the play opens on a light, innocent note, these lines herald the approaching calamity created by Leontes' jealousy that will affect all the characters at the royal court. Both aspects can become visible in set and costume colors: Dark tapestries may hang from the set walls; Hermione wear a soft, deep, sober tone

AS YOU LIKE IT: Sketch for Celia & Rosalind   *Costumes for Rosalind & Celia*

in a single color over a youthful shift, to express her inner serenity, and for Leontes a chaotic mixture of colored paints applied to the fabric of his costume to express his emotional confusion. Further words significant to me were those uttered by the Delphic oracle when asked to pronounce on the question of Hermione's innocence or guilt:

"… and the king shall live without an heir
If that which is lost be not found."

They refer first to the newborn child but also indicate the need of both Leontes and Hermione to find each other again in a new, conscious way, if both inner and outer order is to be restored.

It is also important to be aware of the **turning point** or **climax** of the play. The major turning point in *The Winter's Tale* occurs when the scene changes from the inside world of Sicilia to the open spaces of Bohemia and the season from winter to summer. The dimensions of the transformation these changes herald become apparent in the Old Shepherd's words at the end of Act III:

"…thou met'st with things dying, I with things new born."

These words expressed for me the **central theme**, that of transformation of death into life, of resurrection. It recurs in Paulina's words to Leontes when the statue of his supposedly deceased wife returns to life:

"Bequeath to death your numbness, for from him
Dear life redeems you."

To make visible the transformation of personal turmoil and pain into general joy and redemption, I changed the previous somber colors and textures into light and translucent ones in both set and costumes, using pastel tones in soft fabrics.

4. STUDYING

Other sources of inspiration have been books, essays and lectures. I might mention as examples Charles and Mary Lamb's synopses of Shakespeare's stories and Cecil Harwood's study, *Shakespeare's Prophetic Mind*. Rudolf Stein-

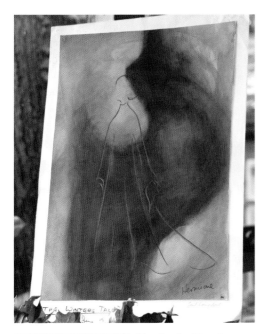

THE WINTER'S TALE: Sketches for Hermione

Paulina

Leontes

er's insights have always opened doors to new understandings of Shakespeare's plays, their characters and the motivation for their actions.

A particular source of inspiration to me has been the fourteenth lecture in the Speech and Drama Course, in which Rudolf Steiner described the sequence of the colors of the rainbow as expression of the human being's journey through different inner moods. These colors and their inner qualities can also be understood as differing ways of perceiving the self and the world.

The cool tones begin the rainbow color sequence and move towards the warm. A mood of prayer can be experienced in the **violet** of immeasurable expanses; this transforms into a **blue** that expresses inner tranquility, and then into the **green** of growing, blossoming nature, so that the eye journeys from distant and invisible worlds to the here and now, with all that can be experienced along the way. When it moves on to the **yellow**, a feeling of self confirmation can arise that the **orange** warms, so that when

the final color has been reached, the **red** awakens a love towards all humanity.

This way of looking at color has become the foundation on which I have built my approach to design. With color as the starting point, I have been led directly into the inner moods or outer atmospheres and then on into the life of the entire story. Color moves freely before it is captured into texture and form or style and speaks to an audience with an immediacy that neither texture nor style can improve on. I never compromise on color even if I have occasionally had to do so in the other areas of design, texture and style.

APPLICATION

1. FINDING COLORS

After arriving at an approach to and vision of the play, I am ready to begin to involve colors in the design. With a blank sheet of paper and the essence of the characters living in color in my

imagination, I paint abstract forms in an attempt to capture the inner reality of each phase of the story. By dipping my brush intuitively into the colors and letting them lead the way, the development of each character becomes the overall composition of the play.

Then I stand back, to see if I can experience the story of the play as what I now call a 'color journey.' If I cannot, I keep working at the journey. When I can, I identify the specific colors and tones in the different parts of the painting that capture the core or essence of the characters and write their names in each area. The next step is to test whether the character colors are effective when placed beside each other in individual scenes. For this I make what I call a 'strip cartoon.' This is a long ribbon of paper, four to six inches high, and of indefinite length. I read each scene in sequence and immediately afterwards with colored pencils draw the essence of each character as movements and forms, not as representational images. If what I have created in any of these previous steps does not 'speak' to me, I repeat the process until it does.

Color collage for THE MERCHANT OF VENICE

Strip cartoon for CYMBELINE

2. EXPLORING TEXTURES

After finding the characters' colors through this process, it is time to find the textures that enhance them in the way they feel, move and catch the light. I have spent many hours in fabric shops, allowing different cloths with varying textures to run through my fingers. I also drape each one over any available furniture to discover which textures most effectively express the essence of the scene or character.

Then I consider the relationship between the color and the texture I have chosen: When the texture speaks the same language as the color of the set or character, both are simple and direct. When texture and color are deliberately in contrast with each other, the situation or character can be made to look complex, even duplicitous. Soft, flowing fabrics on elegant windows or young, fast-moving characters, for example, give them their full potential. The same fabrics in a rough cabin or on an elderly peasant look thin and express either poverty or meanness, making an entirely different state-ment. Likewise, a stiff and unyielding cloth on those fast-moving characters prevents natural movement, and so they appear hard and even cruel.

3. RESEARCHING STYLES

Then it is time to investigate which style enhances the colors and textures chosen so far: Should the play be set in a past or historical period? Does the production need a contemporary look? Does it want to be set in a future or imaginary period? I not only use reference books but go to museums and art galleries, and to towns and cities, to assess the relationship of styles of clothing to architectural styles, when designing set and costumes. I also look at how clothing styles relate to professions and life-styles for costume and character. When entering a cathedral, I have imagined the builders constructing the arches and the craftsmen carving the intricate decorations and seen the quality of the spaces created for specific purposes. Then I have envisaged how they were dressed. I have also visited stately homes to study the details of the period in the building and to visualize the ladies of the same era gliding along the corridors in their elaborate and elegant dresses. Then I imagine how King Lear's castle or the halls, in which Beatrice and Benedick in *Much Ado about Nothing* conduct their courtship battles, might look and how the spaces might be lit.

4. SKETCHING

The most daunting moment has finally arrived. My aim now is to commit the results of the research, images and impressions to paper. It has long been my ideal to do this in such a way that all company members can understand the vision of the play and intention of the design. To help achieve this when sketching, I empathize with each character, giving special attention to the hands. I imagine the individual way in which the character moves his or her hands, so that their positioning in the sketch gives an impression of the personality. I also search for the specific technique or techniques that belong to the vision: Do I draw an outline of the character

Nylon chiffon

Satin

Velvet

first and then fill in the colors? Do I paint a swath of colors and outline the figure on top? Do I cut out the figure in white paper or cloth, to paste onto colored paper? Do I paste the colored figure onto a white background? The possibilities are endless, and whatever my imagination gives me, I may well use not only for the costumes of the character but also for aspects of the set and lighting.

It can be worthwhile not completing the final details when coming to the end of designing. The unfinished sketch allows the creative process to continue in the practical building of set and costumes and then even into the creation of the lighting design, the final element in the production to be realized. Each play has its own artistic laws and each production has its particular social circumstances, and they both ask the designer to be open to them and integrate them into the creative process, with all their practical consequences.

5. CONSIDERING THE AUDIENCE

It is a challenge to arrive at a design that satisfies people sitting in every area of the auditorium, as the audience in the back rows and up in the very top of the theatre have a greater overview but see fewer details, while for those in the front rows, the reverse is true. Colors and shapes in set, costume and lighting need to be clear yet understated, and if the designer achieves this, each spectator will have the freedom to enter the world that the production creates in his or her own individual way.

TO SUM UP:

The creative process starts in the inner life, in the imagination of the designer, where colors live most strongly. The colors then awaken the urge to find the textures. The colors and textures together then ask to be given a style or form. How the designer relates inner imaginings to the necessary objective research, and then transforms fabric, wood, metal and other materials into the **clothing of the play**, is the further subject of this book.

Brigitte, Lara and Matt very kindly modelled some costumes for various chapters and wrote of their experiences in wearing them.

MACBETH: Witches

MEASURE FOR MEASURE: Lucio

AS YOU LIKE IT: Touchstone

II
COLOR

"Hail, many-color'd messenger..."

The Tempest, Act IV, scene 1

When running stage design workshops on color, I have frequently been struck by the way in which participants express their experiences of the different color tones. On the one hand, subjective and often emotional statements emphasize personal likes and dislikes; on the other, there is a genuine recognition of an objective quality in each color that transcends personal opinion. As part of the workshop, I usually scatter over forty silk squares on the floor in patterns relevant to the group and the subject and invite the participants to walk between the squares without speaking. They then begin to explore their own relationship to the individual colors, picking up a square in a color they like and another in one they dislike. After moving and playing with the two for a while, they share comments on the feelings that have arisen during the exploration.

In the final step of the exercise, every participant arranges the silks in a collage that expresses a theme he or she has chosen. When this is finished the whole group studies each collage, trying to sense what the themes might be. To general amazement, the participants' sense of the theme is almost always close to, if not identical with, what the creator had in mind.

The final conversation highlights the differences between the personal feelings that each associates with the colors and their objective qualities.

What is color? From a scientific perspective the different colors can be described as varying wavelengths of light, but our interest here is in

the human and artistic experience that arises out of an objective perception that then awakens feelings. This is a world that a designer will want to explore in depth if a design is to incorporate colors in a way that allows them to both enhance and serve the production.

photo by Alysoun Barrett

THE EFFECTS OF COLOR

Colors are obviously an integral part of nature, but we habitually take them for granted, so a simple imaginative exercise can help to bring us closer to them and their effect. The sky is blue and the grass green, as we know, but what would our experience be of the world and of ourselves if these two colors were suddenly reversed?

The main aspect of color relevant to the work of a designer is that it has an objective reality on the one hand, and on the other it profoundly affects our inner life, whether or not we are conscious of it. The colors found in nature and that arise in an individual's inner life are of a different quality, but they build at the same time an invisible bridge between every aspect of the world around and the world of the human soul, and this bridge enables us to sense ourselves as part of our surroundings. This means that a more conscious experience of color can enhance our experience of both worlds. The main effect of colors on our inner world is that they create and so become an immediate expression of what we might call psychological or soul qualities, such as joy and pain.

Language reflects this relationship: We speak of being **green with envy** or in **a blue mood.** Some event may be to us as **a red rag to a bull**, and we see the world **through rose-tinted spectacles**. Consciously or unconsciously, we associate the broad spectrum of colors with a wide range of feelings or psychological qualities, and knowing what these associations are

can be immensely helpful to the designer when searching for ways to convey the inner qualities of a play or a character. Another aspect of color important for the designer to consider is that, even when the shades or hues are identical, colors can appear as different to the observer. A number of aspects determine the way they are perceived: the places in which the specific color is used, the other colors that are placed beside it, the texture or textures combined with the color, the exact hue and tone of the color.

THE RAINBOW

The designer who chooses to look more attentively at the rainbow—a fragile and almost miraculous natural phenomenon that comes into being only in the dance of sunlight and rain—can find both practical and contemplative aspects in it to explore. What contributes to the beauty of the rainbow is that it is a complete circle, though the ground usually hides the lower half. It is only occasionally possible to see it in its entirety, for example, from an airplane on the clouds below. This circle is perhaps the origin of what are called the three color circles or wheels available to the designer.

The **rainbow** color sequence is known in color theory as an archetypal color wheel and consists of six colors, which are then paired. The three primary colors are **red**, **yellow** and **blue**, and their complementary colors are **green**, **purple** and **orange** respectively. The latter are called complementary colors because when mixed in the proper proportion with the primary color with which they are paired, they produce

one of the neutral colors of varying shades of grey. There are also two other color wheels of colors in either paler or darker tones, the first of **pastel** colors and the second of **earth** colors.

As mentioned earlier, one of my own sources of inspiration has been the way in which Rudolf Steiner described the sequence of colors in the rainbow in the Speech and Drama lectures. The evolving relationship that Steiner set out between the colors of the rainbow and the awakening and development of human consciousness has allowed me to find a way of connecting specific colors to the characters for whom I was designing costumes; I could relate or link their inner development in the course of the play to one or more of the stages in that color sequence.

IN SET AND COSTUMES

One of the first plays for which I began to explore this relationship or correspondence between a color and a character in practice was *The Tempest*: I discovered that Caliban knows all the rivers and plants on his island but very little about himself, and so I dressed him in a costume that had an abundance of greens. I sensed that Prospero's daughter, Miranda, carried within her a future that was full of hope, so I gave her a simple, flowing costume in a mixture of the colors of dawn, soft peach and rose. For the magus Prospero, who I understood to have so deepened his knowledge of nature and of himself that he commands the natural elements, I designed his magic cloak in all the colors of the rainbow as a symbol in color of his magic powers.

After further exploration of the relation of human psychology or consciousness to color, I began to develop this approach, beginning with colors for costumes and, as my first way of differentiating between characters, used the colors found in nature for those that do not know themselves well, and for those with a strong and more conscious inner life, I chose colors that expressed one or more inner aspects of the character.

I also discovered that each color has the capacity to express both the positive and negative of an inner quality in the human being, and which of the two aspects is expressed is determined by the way in which the colored dyes and paints are applied. So I began to use individual colors to express the following psychological qualities that can be applied to both set and costumes, placing violet at the end of the sequence: **blue**: wisdom, humility, tenderness, insipidness; **green**: a love of nature, an out-going quality, little awareness of the self, jealousy; **yellow**: a sense of self-awareness, youthfulness, a lively wit, cruelty; **orange**: cheekiness, spunk, energy, brashness, harshness; **red**: warmth, activity, devotion, anger; **violet** or **purple**: solemnity, reverence, frailty.

The conventional use of individual colors in everyday clothing has been included in this chapter, primarily to indicate how the same colors can be used either in a similar way or differently in costume and set.

COLOR IN LIGHTING

Finally, it is important to note that the principles that determine how color can be used in costume and set do not necessarily apply to color in lighting, because in lighting the three primaries and their complementary colors are different: **red/cyan**, **blue/yellow** and **green/magenta**. Their effects will be addressed in the chapter that deals specifically with lighting.

THE RAINBOW COLORS

1. BLUE

The blue of the sky overhead is our constant companion whenever we find ourselves in the natural world, even when the heavens are cloudy and their color cannot be seen. The blue invites us into the infinite distances of those heavens; they allow us to breathe out, relax, to

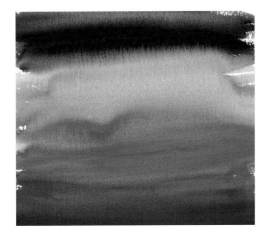

find peace of mind and solace of soul. In terms of traditional color theory, blue is the coolest of the rainbow colors. The strongest effect of blue on the human soul, in all its shades from pale to midnight blue, is that it creates an impression of loyalty and dependability, and when we find blues in the plant world, we perhaps experience them as having the qualities of modesty and delicacy.

In clothing: Beside black, blue is perhaps the most popular color for clothes, as the blue jeans worn by both sexes of all ages all over the world, without barriers of class or climate, exemplify.

In costume: Blue is the color for those characters that are shy, quiet and retiring as well as loyal and selfless; these characters serve others, even if this indicates a weakness. Other psychological qualities of blue are the wisdom of an older character or the innocence of a child or youth. It may give the impression of a character's inability to make decisions. The differentiations between the above are usually expressed by varying the tones; the effect can be heightened by using different fabric textures.

In set: A blue curtain or flat recedes into the background and makes any space larger. Blue in the set can look either noble and uplifting or heavy and dull, depending on the color used in the lighting.

In lighting: Blue is the main color used to create coolness on stage. Blue can appear mysterious and tends to expand the space, as its effect

COLOR : **THE RAINBOW COLORS**

is in scenery. It is difficult to create dark shadows with blue lighting, unless the color comes from isolated lighting instruments. Blue light on blue surfaces of scenery or costume wipes out or nullifies the color and creates a picture with few or no contrasts.

2. GREEN

The color of the plant world and of nature surrounds us at least in some moments of the day and is closer than the blue of the sky. It is the color that has the widest variety of tones and can still be experienced as green, as the great array of greens in springtime and their changes throughout the season demonstrate. Whatever the shade of green, we are usually more aware of its world than of ourselves within it. The green of nature can be calming, and walking through the green tones present in field and forest may refresh us. Where blue meets green, the watery element becomes apparent and creates a cooling quality. Green can be heavy

and dark when the color begins to decay, and this can create a quality of eeriness that awakens anxiety in the observer. At the other end of its spectrum, as a pale and soft tone, green can make us yearn for unknown and open spaces.

In clothing: Green seems to drain the human complexion of color; because of this it may prove difficult to wear. In its pure tone green dominates and so is often found in a tone that leans towards its neighboring color of blue or yellow.

In costume: Using green can illustrate how characters wearing it may be unaware of themselves or of others, both as a strength or weakness. The color may also convey that a character has submitted to outer influences or powers. Cleon, in *Pericles*, when under the evil influence of his wife, is an example. When the green leans towards blue, it lends a quality of nobility to a character. When the green moves into yellow and into an acidic tone, it can convey a character's envy or bitterness.

In set: Green conveys an impression of an outdoor setting, perhaps the country or a parkland. A green space is not as wide or as cool as blue, nor is it as calm, noble or conscious. The color makes a space earthy and familiar. Green can also convey an impression of emptiness.

In lighting: Green lighting can create an impression of a wide-open, cool space. It has a strange way of making the space wider than blue, but not as lofty. Exclusive or a dominant use of the color in lighting creates a bilious effect and in its pure tones is most effective when used spar-

ingly. Green bleaches or washes out other colors on stage.

3. YELLOW

Yellow is always associated with light. Children draw the sun in yellow, and when we look at a yellow surface, we may sense that it has a shining or radiating quality. Psychologically, there is a happy quality to yellow as well as alertness, and when the tone is cooler it hints at sharpness. Yellow bridges the cool and warm colors and so is able to stand alone, as though making visible an individual's self-awareness or intellectual capacities. As a color it wants to spread out, so can be difficult to contain. When blended with other colors, yellow makes a strong and distinct difference to a whole picture.

In clothing: Yellow can express a character's lightness, happiness, honesty or openness. It can also convey loneliness or separateness and, again, in its cooler tones, a hint of aggression.

In costume: Yellow may be a good choice for a character that stands apart, such as a clown or musician. A character that wishes to bridge opposing sides or bring humor and wit to a situation may wear yellow. Yellow can convey an unfeeling or cruel streak in a character. Used carefully, yellow can be a powerful and effective tool to highlight a particular moment in a character's development.

In set: Yellow does not create background spaces and if used in larger quantities overwhelms the actors and their actions. A yellow drape or curtain can lift a dark set. This uplifting effect can be created when a yellow tablecloth or cushion is placed on a table or chair, or when yellow is the color of the flowers in a vase on the table.

In lighting: Yellow light alone is almost impossible to see as a clean light. It makes most fabric surfaces in both costumes and set appear dull and dirty and the complexion of the actors unhealthy or ill.

4. ORANGE

As we now approach the warmer colors, we leave behind the infinite distances encountered in the natural world at the beginning of the journey through the colors and perceive closeness, in orange in particular, as though the glow of yellow has been ignited and created a vibrant and active fire that is continually moving. Orange is a mixture of its neighbors yellow and red and contains the qualities of both radiance and warmth. Psychologically, there is an element of both cheekiness and spunk that orange conveys, and this enlivens any surrounding. It

usually has a joyous quality but can also be experienced as hard or callous and selfish.

In clothing: Orange makes a strong and bold statement, whether this is intended or not, and can be difficult for an individual to wear without being overwhelmed by it. Orange contributes a gregarious quality to any circumstance.

In costume: Orange brings a dynamic quality to a character that can be either positive or negative. The color brings clarity and differentiation to a collage of warm tones and can make a crowd scene alive and active.

In set: Orange creates an indoor atmosphere and adds a companionable quality to a set. The color enlivens a set, and whether used on painted flats or for drapes, furniture or a few scattered cushions, it creates focus.

In lighting: Orange lighting easily makes set and costumes look both hot and indistinct.

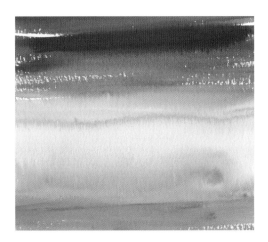

5. RED

Red is the color of the blood that courses through the body and of the heart that is its central organ. The color of the love that flows from individual human beings to everything they may hold dear is conventionally red, as is that of the rose when it is the symbol of that love.

Red is also the color of Mars, the god of war, and the color that appears in our faces when anger arises in us. It is an active and dynamic color: It comes forcefully towards the observer and actively draws attention towards itself. This common understanding has led red to be used in traffic lights when safety demands that we stop. Red has little subtlety or mystery, is direct and makes its own rules. In lighter shades that move either towards pink or towards maroon, it soon loses its directness. Psychologically, it can awaken positive or negative experiences in the observer, depending on the quality of the tone,

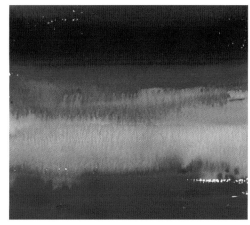

but whatever its quality we are rarely in doubt as to its message.

In clothing: Red has a cheerful and happy appearance and is especially suitable for clothing for young children full of bounce and energy. When looking at a crowd, the reds in the clothing can usually be picked out immediately. To wear red an adult requires confidence, and some individuals may go through life without ever wearing it.

In costume: Red expresses the strong qualities of energy, joy and also anger in a character. The color reveals every aspect of love in a character, both the more and the less virtuous. Red is a powerful tool if used sparingly and only for specific characters in particular moments.

In set: Red always dominates a set. The color creates a more enclosed and intimate quality that may be used for indoor scenes. Red is easier to use as fabric for curtains or drapes than as paint on a flat or on a floor cloth, even when it is blended with other colors.

In lighting: Red in lighting is the most strongly dramatic color in the rainbow. It either washes out all the other colors or makes everything appear angry, usually both. It is effective on a white backdrop or white cyclorama when creating an atmosphere of battle. In lighting, red helps to create sunrises or sunsets.

6. PURPLE

We have now reached the other end of the rainbow and the final color that I have placed in the sequence: purple. It takes us out into the infinite distances again. But the journey through the other colors has taken the observer into intense and dramatic experiences and so has brought change. What was the wisdom that lived in blue can be rediscovered in the color purple, but it has been transformed, and as a psychological quality purple now conveys a reverence for all that is noble and good. Purple can express the inner qualities of dignity and nobility; it also conveys a seriousness that allows an individual to look inward; this may include a tendency towards contemplation or meditation. Purple is a balance between what are conventionally called the warm and cool colors and so can have a quality of objectivity.

In clothing: Purple makes a strong statement, without overwhelming other colors. The color is often used for ecclesiastical garments and royalty. Purple is generally reserved for evening wear and for other special occasions.

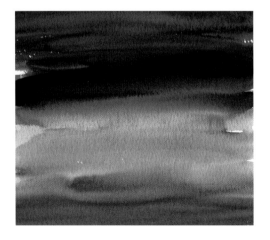

In costume: Purple may emphasize the position or status of kings, queens, priests and other members of the nobility. The color may age the character.

In set: Purple looks dull or grey when applied to the painted surface of a set. The effect of the color is stronger when used in fabrics. Purple is an effective alternative to black when creating a dark atmosphere in a set.

In lighting: Purple brings a quality of solemn or serious beauty to lighting. When the color is created by mixing red and blue, the tone is balanced and allows the shadows to breathe.

THE PASTEL COLORS

Pastel colors are those that we see in the sky at dawn or at dusk, when the light and the dark are in continuous transition as day moves to night or night turns to day. The more delicate tones of these colors create a new color wheel that follows the same sequence as the circle of rainbow colors. This is subtle and can be experienced as mysterious, and the sensations that these colors awaken in the human soul are gentler. The pastel tones echo their brighter sisters in their psychological or inner qualities, but they certainly do not take second place behind the rainbow colors; rather, they have their own distinct and unique role to play in the broader world of colors and their effects.

In costume: Taken in reverse sequence to the above, the soft tones of **lavender** heighten the romantic side of a character; they may also express a character's sorrow or gentle melancholia. The warm tones of **rose** and **peach** allow characters to appear calm and full of love and give them a quiet strength. Dressing characters in any of these three pastel tones emphasizes their youth; they can be effective colors for fairy-tale characters that bring about change in a situation in which renewal is needed. **Pale yellow** balances the warmer and cooler colors and separates characters such as children and troubadours from others. **Greens** and **blues** express a quality of modesty; this can include thoughtfulness and loyalty. Cooler colors usually look dirty and grey under stage lighting; only the textures of the costume fabrics can alter this effect.

In set: All pastel colors give an air of elegance or antiquity to a set. If the paleness of the colors is extreme, the set may appear dusty and neglected. Pastel colors are useful when the bolder rainbow or earth colors are too powerful or strong.

In lighting: Pastel colors in lighting enable changes in atmosphere or inner quality to be subtle and unobtrusive. They can change from an indoor to an outdoor setting or from warmth to coolness, dullness to brightness or murkiness to clarity; any weather and any time of the day can be created without the audience's noticing.

THE EARTH COLORS

Just as the pastel colors are present in the sky and evoke seasonal and weather effects, the earth colors are present in the soil and vegetation and also the man-made environment. In everyday life earth colors are suitable for the working clothes of craftsmen and land workers. Artists love to paint with earth colors: Being within their own color circle, they are subdued and blend easily in their subtle variations.

In costume: The earthiness of the color can express a character's earthiness, suggesting

great practicality but also a possible dullness. When dressed in **grey/blue** or **sage/olive green**, a character can almost vanish while on stage and thus convey his or her modesty. These colors can also convey weakness or shiftiness in a character. **Lime/green yellow** can make a sharp wit visible; it also expresses jealousy or spite. The warmer hues of **yellow ochre** and **rust/orange** enhance a character's liveliness and sense of fun. In **reds** and **browns** the liveliness can grow in strength and may be used for a domineering character.

In set: Earth colors create a strongly rustic feel in the space, with the cooler tones creating an outdoor environment and the warmer ones the space of a cabin or woodland cottage. Homespun or roughly woven drapes and rugs may enhance this atmosphere.

In lighting: Earth colors in lighting blend well with the pastel colors. They can be too dark for the stage and distort the actors' complexions.

BLACK

As the ultimate in darkness, black creates a mysterious and somber mood that may feel threatening to the observer. The color has a sobering effect and can therefore create an atmosphere of objectivity and elegance. When used as part of the background, black throws lighter objects into sharp relief; the color can also swallow the darker ones.

In clothing: Black is a color many wear as city or office clothing. The clergy of many religions

and members of many religious communities, as well as police and fire services, orchestras and choirs all wear black. Black is conventionally worn at funerals, perhaps because it gives mourners a feeling of security at a time of uncertainty. The color gives an individual a strong sense of self.

In costume: A black costume against a black background can create an empty space on the stage. The color can heighten the seriousness of a character. It can also express the darkness in a criminal's evil intent.

In set: Black is usually most effective when used in special situations. The color can make a scene more serious than necessary because colored lighting cannot change the atmosphere black creates. Even when painted under other colors, black pigment shows up under the lights and remains black.

In lighting: Black can be used only for black-outs. Black light is another name for ultraviolet or UV lighting, and when it is used to light ultraviolet paint in a blacked-out scene on stage, it creates a phosphorescent effect.

WHITE

White is the ultimate in lightness; color seems to have left it entirely, and yet it is still a color. The color's sharpness and brightness can also have an unpleasant, perhaps blinding effect on the observer. As its psychological qualities, white expresses simplicity, purity and an open honesty, so that nothing remains hidden. In contrast to black, white blends well with other colors close by, as though striving for harmony. It absorbs their tones and can reflect other colors nearby.

In clothing: White is the color most used for clothing worn closest to the skin, as the color creates a feeling of safety. Young girls wear the color for their confirmation and young women in the Western world for their weddings. Nurses, chefs and many sportsmen and sportswomen wear white uniforms. In summer, holiday crowds in white have a light and airy appearance.

In costume: White brings freshness to any costume, whether it is a shirt, an underskirt or a frilled cuff or collar. When an entire overgarment is white, the color dominates. When combined with white, different fabrics and their textures have different effects: Silks shine or may glare. Wool and velvet soften the intensity of the color.

In set: White scenery has a stark effect until colored lights add layers that give depth to the base.

In lighting: The shine of white lighting can create a quality of purity on the stage. The color has a coldness that can make the shadows dramatic. Strong white lighting can glare and blind the audience.

GREY

Grey is created when black and white, or dark and light, are mixed. When no other colors are added to the mixture, the color created has a neutral and objective quality. Grey can also be created by mixing complementary colors unevenly; this method gives the tone a richer and more subtle quality. One of the color's characteristics is that it swallows light and so can look drab in any of the three elements of design, in costume, scenery and lighting.

In clothing: As a mixture of white and black, grey retains its neutral quality without succumbing to either the somber quality of black or the lightness of white.

In costume: In costume the color can give a character a puritanical appearance that can be heightened when combined with straight lines and simple forms. Soft, flowing fabrics in grey can give an elegance to an elderly character.

In set: If the color is the main one used in a set, it creates an atmosphere of isolation or grief that may create eeriness on stage.

In lighting: Grey in lighting dulls any space and imbues it with coolness, even heaviness.

CONTRASTS IN COLOR

Each color has a strongly individual quality in whichever color wheel it is at home, but without others as contrasts any main color may become too dominant, so the designer's creativity starts when bringing individual colors together. In both costume and scenery it is obvious that many colors are needed.

In costume: A costume can be either full of contrasts to emphasize the contradictions in a complex character, or they can be softly blended to express either a character's inner harmony or the same character's blandness or lack of inner color.

In set: A set that consists mainly of blended colors may allow the scenery to remain in the background. If the colors are bold and contrasted, the set may dominate the stage.

In lighting: A set lit either strongly or subtly by contrasting colors can create both strong and subtle shadows, giving depth and variety to a space. A set lit with one dominant color creates an evenness and harmony in a space, but may also create an atmosphere of monotony.

FINAL THOUGHTS

When a designer begins to work consciously with colors, he or she will soon discover that they offer unlimited possibilities, and the designer can be tempted to either work slowly and carefully, experimenting freely and at leisure, or to splash out with them intuitively, working quickly and boldly. Since both can be essential elements in a creative design process, it is a matter of finding the colors and tones and combinations that have the capacity to express what the designer wishes to express of the inner and outer life of individual characters, scenes and acts and of the entire story of the play.

III

TEXTURES

"Costly thy habit as thy purse can buy,

But not express'd in fancy; rich, not gaudy;

For the apparel oft proclaims the man."

Hamlet, Act I, scene 3

The most intriguing costume I have ever seen was in the wardrobe at the Stuttgart Opera House, where I had been sent on placement during my training. One of my tasks was to hang away all the costumes no longer in use up in an attic space that seemed to me the size of a football field. Each costume had a five- or six-digit number that I had to use to guide me to its home, and while I was plowing my way through the racks one day, looking for the right space for one particular costume, I came across a garment in Elizabethan style that was made entirely of calico. It was painted with dyes and oils in a variety of techniques. Different shades of dye were used to distinguish the overdress from the underskirt, which also had brocade patterns painted on it. The cloak had been sprayed with sawdust that had previously been soaked in glue so that it looked like velvet, and holes had been cut in a particular pattern into a strip of the calico at the neck and wrists to create the impression that the garment had lace frills. When I asked about the origin of this costume, I was told that during World War II the wardrobe had had nothing but calico out of which to make costumes, so the costume builders had had to use their ingenuity. This costume has inspired me ever since because it taught me a level of inventiveness that has been essential to my stage work and has stood by me through many restricted budgets and uncharted scenarios.

MATERIALS

If the design process begins with color, the textures used for scenery and costume bridge the colors that have already been chosen and the style still to be determined. Alongside the colors, the surfaces of materials used on stage, such as **wood**, **metal** and **fabric**, all help to create and express the moods of the production so that the inner life of the story and of the characters becomes a sensory experience for the audience. The textures contribute to this experience by absorbing and then reflecting the light in different ways. The main contrast in textures

as the outer expression of inner worlds is between those that are rough and uneven and those that are smooth. However, textures in set and textures in costume work differently, for a simple reason: Those of the scenery stay in one place, while those of the costumes move with the actors and can help or hinder their actions. So it is essential to explore and then familiarize oneself with the different properties of each texture. Their individual qualities and the interplay between set and costumes can then be used most effectively. Any lighting textures, such as those created by gobos, can be added at a later stage in the design process, once the textures for set and costumes have been chosen.

WOOD

Wood is a useful material for building scenery as it is easy to cut to any shape and attach in unlimited ways. Hard woods are more durable and soft woods easier to handle. However, wood is heavy, has weakness at the notches and is inclined to warp. On view to the audience its textural surface can be rough or smooth, depending on how it is finished. When rough its splinters catch any passing costume cloth, but when lit it looks warm and almost velvety. When the wood is smooth it can gain a shiny surface, even reflect the light and be altogether more elegant when painted.

METAL

Metal is strong and heavy and used for hanging lighting units and supports for bulkier scenery that has to carry heavy weights. Lighter metals such as aluminum can be used for structural purpose and often comes with ready-made holes for assembling. Cutting and re-joining heavier metal involves welding tools. When used as scenery in view of the audience, the textures are rough, even rusty or high gloss when polished, catching the light with dazzle.

FABRIC

Two elements create the texture of a fabric: the **fiber** and the **weave**. How the two elements combine determines the way in which the fabric behaves or moves, and particular combinations of fiber and weave can be strongly expressive in both set and costumes. A light and lively character, such as Ariel in *The Tempest*, may wear a soft, light and flowing fabric, such as chiffon. A more self-centered and therefore enclosed character, such as Antiochus in *Pericles*, may wear a stiff, unyielding cloak, perhaps made of linen or a firm synthetic or metallic fiber, which provides him with the means to close himself off from others when necessary.

To research textures most effectively, I suggest what may seem obvious: using the principle of trial and error. When the designer takes the time to experiment with different pieces of cloth in different ways—draped over a piece of static furniture or hung as a drape or pinned to the body of an actor moving in character—and then studies the effects under colored lights, it is possi-ble to find a texture that truly creates the desired effect. However, not all designers have enough fabrics at their disposal in the textures and colors needed, so the following are general indications on the effects of the fibers and weaves of fabrics in set and costumes and under lighting.

FABRIC FIBERS

There is a marked difference between **natural** and **man-made** fibers, and each fulfills its own particular role on the stage. Natural fibers are kinder to the wearer and softer to the eye but generally less hard-wearing than the man-made ones. Man-made fibers are dense and tend to look less alive under the lights, but are gener-ally less expensive. The ongoing development of new synthetic fabrics continues to diminish the differences between the two.

1. NATURAL FIBERS

WOOL: This is a natural animal fiber from the backs of sheep, goats and camels and is well-known for its warmth because it regulates body heat more effectively than most fabrics. The minute hooks on each hair give it a springiness and resilience and allow it to keep its shape well, but when these are roughly treated, they usually tangle and cause the fabric to shrink. This rough treatment is a technique intentionally used to make felt; through this process it becomes thicker and more hard-wearing.

In set: Woolen curtains, blankets, cushions and rugs lend a pleasant and warming indoor quality to a set. **In costume:** As a fabric, wool generally looks heavy and can give the wearer an older, dignified appearance, while tired or downtrod-den characters may appear melancholy or impoverished when dressed in it. Wool used for costumes in crowd scenes softens the overall effect. On a practical note, woollen fabrics are particularly warm when actors wear them under stage lighting, so it is advisable to restrict their use. **In lighting:** The fabric surface absorbs the stage light, making it easier for the character to blend into the background.

SILK: This natural animal fiber has almost the opposite properties to wool. The silkworm spins

Wool

Wool

its cocoon in one long, fine thread, and the thread from the inner part of the cocoon makes a fine, strong and smooth fabric. When cloth is woven with thread from the outer layers, the texture of the silk fabric is rougher and has irregularities. Silks dye well into radiant colors, but these are difficult to fix permanently.

In set: Silk hangings and furniture covers bring an air of elegance and femininity to a set. **In costume:** Silk moves fluidly around and over the actor's body, giving the wearer a feeling of suppleness and luxury. It also has a unique sheen which makes the fabric appear delicate and pure. A quality of richness is added when the silk is woven into elaborate designs. **In lighting:** Finer silk reflects the stage lighting and

can therefore dazzle the audience, but fabrics woven from the rougher fibers absorb the light and appear dull.

LINEN: Sometimes known as flax, linen is a natural plant fiber similar to its close relatives, **hemp** and **sisal**. They all belong to the range of fabrics used to make sails and sacks, for example, because of their strength and weight. One of the attractions of linen is that its woven structure is clearly visible; this includes its occasional irregularities.

In set: Linen, hemp and sisal lend themselves to rustic environments, such as woodland cabins, and to outdoor settings. They are also useful for 'scrunching' over a base made of wood and

wire to create rocks or other irregular structures; this irregular linen surface can be painted in the same way as flats and other scenery. **In costume:** Linen can be stubbornly rigid or flow freely, depending on the density of the weave and the cut of the garment. The natural weight of linen ensures that it hangs well but creases easily. The qualities it lends the wearer lie between wool and silk and may work well for down-to-earth characters. **In lighting:** Because it creases easily, the angular patterns of the creases create sharp shadows under stage lighting that can be used to create strong dramatic effects.

COTTON: Cotton is another natural plant fiber that grows in a pod around the seeds and has a

Top: Silk   *Bottom: Japanese silk*   *Top: Raw Silk*   *Bottom: Jacquard silk*   *Linen*

soft and fluffy appearance. It has countless uses, depending on how it is woven. When used on stage it has a neutral quality and is durable and resilient to all sorts of rough treatment, so it is popular for both set and costumes. Cotton is generally finer than linen, feels comfortable against the skin and regulates body temperature. Like linen, it creases, and its lighter weight and slightly rough surface make it hard to drape. However, it is easy to dye and paint.

In set: Finer cotton makes good tablecloths and other interior decorations. It can also be used for painted or embroidered screens that need to be semi-transparent. **In costume:** The thinner, looser and the interlock cotton weaves are ideal for shirts, blouses and undergarments. Heavy

Top: Cotton   *Bottom: Poplin*

cotton fabrics also make imposing period skirts that hold their shape well. **In lighting:** The effect of cotton fabric lies somewhere between wool and silk and varies according to its weave. As a principle, the rougher the surface, the more light it absorbs and the duller it appears.

2. SYNTHETIC OR MAN-MADE FIBERS

Acrylic, nylon, polyester and many other synthetic fibers are made from mineral substances and processed in specialized ways. They crease less than natural fibers but are difficult to dye and paint. However, man-made fabrics drape well and in the main hold their shape.

In set: Man-made furnishing fabrics have a substantial weave and can be heavy to handle. They do not take paint as well as natural cloth, but are more hard-wearing. **In costume:** Synthetic fibers tend to have greater definition and thus lend themselves to enhancing extremes. The glass-like fabric used in a costume made for Lady Macbeth illustrates her cold nature. The extreme lightness or heaviness of man-made fibers can also convey the essence of Shakespeare's supernatural worlds. **In lighting:** The surfaces of many synthetic fabrics are hard and reflect the light more than they absorb.

3. FABRIC WEAVES

BROCADE: Brocade is made from many colored threads of silk, cotton or synthetic fibers interwoven in intricate patterns. It has a rich and opulent texture, and there are few fabrics that look so luxurious. It is usually a heavy and unyielding fabric, which makes it bulky for draping.

In set: Brocade cushions and curtains give a quality of luxury to any setting. **In costume:** Brocade pleats well and easily, so it can be used for skirts over crinolines. If the pleats are made to hang from a yoke or collar, they make the cloak or coat full and expansive. **In lighting:** When colored lighting plays on the colored silk threads of brocade, its rich textures are enriched.

BROIDERY or BRODERIE ANGLAISE: As the name suggests, this fabric, usually available in a light weave, is embroidered in a wide variety of motifs in thread that has the same color as the cloth. Small holes are usually cut into the fabric and then embroidered, and these create a lace-like effect.

In set: Broidery or broderie anglaise is best used for window dressing and delicate furnishings to create a setting with a feminine atmosphere. **In costume:** Women's light summer dresses, blouses, aprons and bonnets become more feminine when made of broidery anglaise, while for male characters, ruffs and cuffs made

Brocade

from it give the costume a refined touch. **In lighting:** This fabric is semi-transparent and partially lets through light, so it acquires a subtle glow under lighting.

BUCKRAM: This material is made from plain, woven cotton or sisal and heavily stiffened with glue; the most rigid version comes in two or more layers that have been glued together. It is not conventionally seen on the surface of a costume or set because it is used as a stiffener or backing.

In set: Buckram may be used to strengthen fabrics that need to hold a particular form for an element of set, such as a pelmet for window dressing. **In costume:** Buckram creates a base

on which to build hats, crowns, belts or any other part of a costume requiring a firm backing. **In lighting:** The cloth that covers buckram appears flat under lighting.

CALICO: Calico is made from unbleached cotton and comes in a variety of weights. If left unwashed, it retains some of the natural plant sap that is visible in the fabric as black specks, so that the cloth remains firm. When ironing several layers sewn together, the sap binds the calico to a firm fabric useful as a less firm replacement for buckram. Once washed it becomes softer but does not lose its body entirely. No backstage workshop is complete without a good supply of calico.

In set: When stretched across a wooden frame, the heavier calicoes make excellent flats and serve well as a base that can then be painted. On the other hand, the cloth can be difficult to drape for curtains, for example, because it creates angles in its folds. **In costume:** Calico is a good choice of fabric as backing for fragile cloth when bodices need to be tight or jackets to have a firm shape. Rustic clothing, petticoats and crinolines with frills over the bottom hoop are usually made of calico. **In lighting:** The surface of the cloth is rough and under the lights looks dull and colorless, but this gives it a rustic quality.

CHIFFON: This fabric is woven from either fine silk or synthetic fibers. It is semi-transparent, light and flowing and drapes easily, so that the forms it creates lend beauty and lightness to the wearer. When the silk version is dyed, the colors are radiant. The cloth appears to shrink when wet, but careful ironing returns it to its full size and makes it translucent. If made of pure silk, however, the weave of chiffon is sensitive and snags and tears easily.

In set: Because of its delicacy chiffon is best used as window dressing or light drapes to furniture. **In costume:** This fabric is an ideal choice for costumes for fast and lightly moving characters, such the fairies in *A Midsummer Night's Dream*, or elegant negligees. **In lighting:** How chiffon responds under lighting depends on whether it is made from silk or the harder and flatter synthetic fibers, the silk version appearing more alive and dynamic than the man-made one.

Broderie Anglaise

Top: Buckram   *Bottom: Calico*

CHINTZ: Chintz is a closely woven cotton fabric that is usually printed with elaborate floral designs and then heavily glazed to create a shiny surface. It is hard-wearing and used mainly for furnishings.

In set: Chintz can be an effective fabric for the set, but the floral prints make it advisable to select carefully where and when it is used. However, it can be painted over to defuse the basic design. **In costume:** When broken down with dyes and paints, chintz can be useful in specific period productions, for example, to lend seventeenth century dresses a note of elegance. **In lighting:** The surface sheen can make chintz harsh under stage lighting and create bright reflections.

CREPE: Similar to chiffon but heavier, crepe is made from fine silk or synthetic fibers. It has an elastic quality created by the technique of over-spinning the yarn that gives it a languid flow, but it is difficult to hold still, so is difficult to cut and sew. Crepe is often manufactured with a satin backing that gives it greater stability.

In set: The shiny side of the fabric offers a good contrast to the duller side and so makes it suitable for patchwork designs that need to retain the same base color. Large quantities make elegant window dressing, while in smaller quantities crepe can be used for sets that have an inherently languid or seductive quality, such as a bedroom or a brothel. **In costume:** A lighter version of the cloth, called crepe de Chine or Chinese silk, was a fashionable dress fabric in the 1920s. It was often cut on the bias so that the fabric clung to the body and the dress highlighted the body's curves. It is useful for elegant evening wear, as both her dress and his cloak. **In lighting:** As chiffon, crepe can be made from silk or synthetics, and so how it responds under stage light depends on which fiber has been used to make the costume or set piece. The silk

fabric usually appears more mobile than the synthetic.

JERSEY & OTHER KNITTED FABRICS: These fabrics, made of natural or man-made fibers, have a unique structure, in which one thread continually interlocks with itself in an extra-fine knitted weave. This enables the fabrics to freely stretch and move in any direction. They drape well but do not always retain their shape over time. When being cut, jersey and other knitted fabrics need to be draped either on a dummy or on the actor, as when lying flat the cloth behaves differently than when it hangs vertically.

In set: Jersey may be used for draped curtains but is less suitable for static parts of the set as it does not reliably hold its form unless soaked in sizing or glue. **In costume:** Undergarments and T-shirts are traditionally made of cotton jersey. A heavier jersey is more suitable for costumes with intricate gathers or deep folds, as the structure enables the cloth to swing freely when the actor moves; finer jersey has a tendency to cling to itself. **In lighting:** How jersey and other

Top: Chiffon   *Bottom: Chintz*   *Crepe de Chine*   *Jersey*

knitted fabrics absorb or reflect light depends on which fiber has been used in the making and whether it is a heavy or light weight. The lighter variety appears flat, whereas the heavy jersey may appear rich in texture.

LACE: Lace is a delicate fabric woven from many threads, either natural or man-made, that all interlink in many directions. Different thicknesses of thread are often used to enhance the main motifs in the design. Today lace can be woven in any width, ranging from narrow ribbons to fabrics with a standard width measurement.

In set: As with broidery anglaise, lace heightens the feminine appearance of a set, adding a particular quality of beauty. It may appear as a delicate edge to cushions, dressing table cloths or drapes at windows. **In costume:** Fine lace is not robust enough for full costumes; it is more suited for delicate trimmings at the neck and arms, for both male and female characters. Heavier lace can be used to make a full costume but, because it is semi-transparent, needs to be

backed with a denser fabric. This then creates an opportunity to use contrasting colors. **In lighting:** Lighting enhances the motifs of the lace, as the spaces between the patterns appear dark on the stage.

NET: Net is a fabric woven from several threads that interlink diagonally; this particular weave creates the holes. The fabric is then treated with chemical solutions to give it more body or stiffness. It is made in different weights and can be used in both scenery and costume.

In set: Net is a fabric ideally suited for backdrops and scrims; its transparency creates a space on stage that remains hidden until it is lit. If the scrim is made of natural fibers, it absorbs paint more easily, but is then less hard-wearing and can tear. **In costume:** Net is used mainly to stiffen such undergarments as a petticoat or ballet tutu. If sewn in frills with many layers, it can create the effect of a crinoline. **In lighting:** Because net is the most transparent fabric available, it is almost invisible under lighting unless

there are many layers of it. Any hole in a scrim will show up as a black spot.

ORGANDY: Organdy is another fine, semi-transparent silk or cotton fabric. The fibers are spun into a hard thread, and when woven it behaves like paper and is therefore unsuitable for draping. In addition, it crumples easily and then goes limp, and so requires frequent ironing.

In set: Organdy can act as a scrim, but its denser weave makes the images behind it appear indistinct. It has a limited range of large-scale uses in a set, though finer props such as ladies' small bags and delicate hat decorations can be made from it. **In costume:** When organdy is used to make an over-dress, it can give the character a delicate appearance. It is also a useful fabric for stand-up frills and collars, but larger collars need to be under-wired. **In lighting:** Forms made in organdy appear hard and flat under lights, so it is advisable to use the fabric sparingly if it has not been treated with paints or dyes.

Lace

Costume net

Scenery net

SATIN or SATEEN: This is the name given to fabrics whose main characteristic is their shiny surface. The effect is created by the predominance of the warp threads on the upper surface of the fabric. It drapes well, is stable and is useful for many purposes.

In set: Satin works well for curtains and other set elements that need flow and a sheen as their main qualities. **In costume:** Satin was a favorite dress-making fabric in the past. Its dense weave and glossy appearance make it suitable for elegant costumes that can be worn by self-assured characters. **In lighting:** Lighting heightens the glamorous effect of satin.

TAFFETA: Taffeta is a densely woven fabric made either from natural or synthetic fibers. It has body, so it holds its own shape and rustles as it moves because the folds rub against each other. It is seldom to be found in printed or woven patterns, but the single colors have a rich, soft glow.

In set: The heavier varieties of taffeta can be made into curtains and cushions that have a full and rich quality. **In costume:** Taffeta is ideal for period skirts and dresses worn over crinolines and for gentlemen's waistcoats. It is more effective and less bulky when pleated at the waist of the skirt rather than gathered. A bodice made of taffeta holds its shape well but will be more hard-wearing when given a calico backing. **In lighting:** Stage lighting heightens the richness and glow of taffeta.

VELVET & VELVETEEN: Both these fabrics have a pile and are made from silk, cotton or synthetic fibers. The unique weaving technique uses an extra warp thread that is looped over a rod and then cut to create the pile, similarly to the way in which a carpet is woven. As a result, the surface of the fabric has depth, the silks are shiny and the cotton has a deep warm dullness even when the color is cool. Most velvet fabrics have a nap, which means that the pile leans in one direction. This appears to change the fabric's color when it is laid in different directions. Crushed velvet uses the nap by flattening it in a variety of directions. All velvets are difficult to sew unless the pieces are well-pinned together, because the pile 'walks' or slides around. These fabrics have a good weight and move in a flattering way. They are also an excellent foil for other textures, especially when the design requires that the colors remain unchanged.

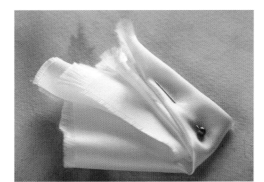

Top: Organdy   *Bottom: Satin*   *Taffeta*   *Top: Crushed velvet*   *Bottom: Velvet*

In set: The three-dimensional quality of velvet adds depth and richness to any curtains or cushions. In deep colors they may create a masculine effect, ideal for the scene of a study. **In costume:** Velvet adds dignity and stature to any style of costume, especially when combined with silky or brocade textures. **In lighting:** Under stage lighting velvet absorbs any brightness and creates shadows that have a strong glow.

In set: The sheen of metallic fabric may appear flat. However, if it is partially painted over, the surface glitter can be transformed into a hidden glow, giving the fabric a new level of life. **In costume:** For characters whose main quality is either their cruelty or their kindness, metallic fabrics can emphasize either their brittle rigidity or inner radiance. Metallic threads in a brocade weave lend opulence to the garment made with

it. These fabrics can also be useful for stage jewelery, crowns and armor. **In lighting:** When paint is applied to the surface sheen of metallic fabrics, either to create patterned motifs or to tone down the brightness of the reflection, the interplay with lighting can create unexpected and powerful effects. With these fabrics it is advisable to experiment with their effects well in advance.

4. METALLIC FABRICS

All metallic fabrics have a fine chemical or aluminum surface coating, either on the fibers before they are woven, on the finished cloth or on both. This creates a sharp, mirror-like sheen. They are cold and hard in appearance, but extremely effective if the designer wants to draw attention to the character or particular part of the set. When placed alongside other softer fabrics, they can add richness and depth to a set or costume.

Corduroy

Metallics

IV
STYLE & FORM

"I think he bought his doublet in Italy,

his round hose in France, his bonnet in Germany,

and his behavior everywhere."

The Merchant of Venice, Act I, scene 2

During a dress rehearsal of Beethoven's *Fidelio*, when I was supposed to be checking the costumes, I became absorbed in one particular scene in which, singing to the glory of the sun, the prisoners slowly emerged from their cells. The setting was a bleak, harshly-edged courtyard surrounded by bleached stone walls. Each prisoner was wearing thin, dirty rags that had long lost their color; only the prison warden and Fidelio herself were better dressed, though the tones of their clothing were also muted. Hearing that the prisoners had been released without his permission, Pizarro, the prison governor, stormed onto the stage. He was dressed in a scarlet uniform with gold epaulettes and braiding that created a stark and jarring contrast to the set and the other costumes. The limp, monotone clothing and harsh enclosure exaggerated the plight of the prisoners, while the rigid style of the governor's uniform emphasized the inflexibility in his character.

When the lights go up for the first time on a production, the audience's eyes are immediately led to the stage space in which the forms and lines of the set prepare them for the story the actors are about to tell. In those first few seconds, the designer has the opportunity to convey the general quality of the play and the period in which it is set. The tool available to achieve this is the style and form of set, costume and lighting. In searching for the style and form of these three elements, the designer needs to consider which past, present, future or purely imaginary styles can best illustrate and express the overall theme of the production.

Just as a costume clothes the body of the actor, so the set clothes the body of the whole play; scenery, furnishings and properties are comparable to the costumes of the characters. **Dress** for the costume and **architecture** for the set

are what will mainly interest and then serve the designer in the search for style. More arts, however—sculpture, painting, literature and music—also reveal how people lived, felt and thought at particular times. In fact, all arts can be understood as expressions of a particular quality of human consciousness and so incorporated into any research for the design of a play. The relationships between dress and architecture through the ages, however, are the main concern for the designer.

King Lear and *Hamlet* demonstrate how the historical setting can be transcended to reveal the play's inner core by the choice of style and form of the set, and then how, if the style and form of costumes of the age in which the play is set are also transformed, the design can express the individual journey of the character from one state of consciousness to another. For example,

in his belief that it is right to bequeath his kingdom to the daughter professing to love him most, King Lear demonstrates a level of innocence that he quickly regrets. The soaring vaults and the soft, flowing lines of dress typical of the Middle Ages lend themselves to the expression of King Lear's lack of insight into human nature, which also determines the atmosphere of his kingdom, because this style creates a sense of simplicity. From the moment that Hamlet learns that his father has been murdered, the prince displays a sharp intelligence as he searches for proof of his uncle's guilt, even if he is compelled to be slow to act. Airy columns, perfectly proportioned arches and marble floors in geometric patterns all create the space for the manifold activities of his capacity for sharp thinking typical of the Renaissance era. Strong, clear-cut pleating that emphasizes the uprightness of the human stature, belts and yokes that draw the eye to the horizontal line, tights that give great freedom of movement and cloaks that fly in any direction all characterize the Renaissance style of dress. This style reveals a strength and clarity in the emerging human intellect.

DRESS & COSTUME

The following ways of looking at the form of the human body can help to determine the style of the costumes. They can aid in the design of both historical styles and new, imaginary ones that express the inner life of the characters.

1. POLARITY

One of the principles determining the styles that have evolved through the ages is the polarity of the naked and the clothed body. Familiar to us from ancient Greek sculptures, the free-flowing folds that were created from gauze-like lengths of cloth indicate that, at that time, clothing with little structure and form was desired, so that the human body, perfect in its propor-

tions, could express a total freedom of movement. The elaborate decorations on layers of padded brocade found on the beautiful and elegant fitted jackets and dresses of the Elizabethans are examples of a desire to reshape or disguise the body.

Within each age there is another creative tension at work: It exists between the general convention and individual taste, between the dictates of fashion (including the uniformity of the professional clothing) and the desire for free expression that creates an entirely individual appearance. This tension is what brings about every new style of dress.

2. THE GOLDEN SECTION

The Golden Section, sometimes known as the Golden Mean, is a proportion that is created by dividing a distance in such a way that the proportion of the smaller section to the larger is the same as the proportion of the larger section to the whole. The Golden Section or Mean is found throughout the human body, although, of

course, all human beings have their own unique variations of it. For example, the proportion of the upper to the lower arm is the same as the proportion of the lower arm to the whole when measured from the fingertips to the shoulder.

The more the Golden Section or Mean is a basis for design, the more harmonious the design becomes. For example, when designing clothing for Portia in *The Merchant of Venice*, whose clear thinking, compassion and capacity for action give her the means to resolve what appears to be an insoluble conflict, the costume designer may choose to work with this principle of balance.

In contrast, the deliberate distortion of the Golden Section can express the opposite. Shylock's obsessive desire for revenge makes clear that reason plays little part in either his thinking or his actions, and his costume may reflect his lack of balance by having distorted proportions. Costumes for Shakespeare's comic characters offer a wide range of opportunities to vary and distort the Golden Section.

3. THE PERSONALITY

Four different types of human personality that are known as the four **temperaments** may be made visible in four basic body shapes. A tall, slender body may have an air of inwardness and **melancholia**. In *As You Like It*, plain, vertical lines and drapes may emphasize the heavy-heartedness of Jaques, an outsider who's deepest love is for philosophy. A short, rounded body evokes a fiery, impetuous and **choleric** nature. In *The Winter's Tale*, padded hips and bust help to create rounded lines for Paulina, who even as a servant is not afraid to set herself against the king. A petite body with quick and agile movements may house a butterfly brain and happy, **sanguine** personality. The use of chaotic, diagonal lines in the costume can emphasize the quick-wittedness and nimble fingers of the pickpocket Autolycus in *The Winter's Tale*. A heavy body with a slow and casual gait can express a placid, easy-going and **phlegmatic** personality. In *The Merchant of Venice*, an absence of clear lines in a loose, floppy gown can help to create the impression that Shylock's

servant, Launcelot Gobbo, tends to be slovenly and has a wavering conscience.

4. THE BODY

Every play has a cast of characters whose actions reveal their strengths and weaknesses, and how the characters are costumed can give them expression. Strength in one area may indicate weakness in another and this, too, may be incorporated into the costume design. One way to do this is to consider where the strength of a particular character lies. It may be in the clarity of **intellect** and capacity to reflect. Hamlet's undoubted strength lies in his capacity for reflection, his weakness is his inability to act. It may lie in the force of **purpose** and capacity to act. King Lear has a capacity to act spontaneously, but he cannot think through the consequences of his actions. It may be found in the warmth of **emotions** and capacity to empathize. Cordelia, King Lear's youngest daughter, has such empathy and steadfastness that it empowers her to withstand her father's actions, but she is not able to think on her feet in moments of crisis.

Intellect and our capacity for reflection are centered in the **head**, and a cool head is considered to be the equivalent of clear thinking. The rounded shape of the head that sits in stillness on the shoulders crowns the human form, and its natural costume is hair. If the intellect is the character's strong point and he or she is of a philosophical bent, then the costuming of the head can be sober and clear in design. A lively and frivolous character, such as a clown, troubadour or courtesan, can carry off a frothy cre-

ation with frills and other adornments. Kings and queens have always been recognizable by their crowns, which represent the unique connection of these human beings to the invisible world of the gods. The actual crown, which allowed them to receive the inspiration needed to serve their people, was originally a simple circle of gold that rested on the brow and remained open to what streamed down on them from above; in later times the crown's center became closed when a new consciousness evolved. Hamlet's princely birth and noble mind might suggest a simple, slender band of gold as a crown, whereas King Lear's foolish hot-headedness might earn him an upside-down crown.

Purpose and our capacity to act lives in our **limbs**; their many muscles and joints allow and invite us to move freely, in contrast to the normal resting position of the head. The way in

Temperaments

which our **legs** are formed enables us to stand firmly on the ground yet step with confidence in any direction at a moment's notice, leaving the arms free to perform more creative actions. When the legs are enveloped in many layers of cloth, the actor's movements are restricted and the overall impression created is of a heaviness and unwillingness to act. King Lear may be clothed in a long, thick gown that draws attention to the way in which the costume hampers his impulsive movements at the opening of the play. In contrast, full sleeves, gathered at the wrist, emphasize the movement of the arms. The **hands**, as the most subtle instruments of human action, enable us to give and to take. Hands and fingers are the tools of the craftsman and can carry out the most intricate movements and achieve extremely complex tasks. Clothing for both arms and legs that allows for as much freedom of movement as possible expresses an energetic and fired sense of purpose. To draw

attention to the fact that at the start of the play Hamlet cannot make use of the freedom that his status gives him, he may be clothed in tights.

Emotions are at home in the middle region of the body, the trunk; its center, the heart and the lungs, bridges the head and the limbs. This part of the body needs warmth and protection for the many organs housed there that are vital to life. Of all areas characterized so far, this is the most sensitive. The rhythmical beat of the heart and the rise and fall of the lungs continually adapt and change as they strive for balance in their interaction, and the emotions ebb and flow, rise and fall, in the same way. This dynamic exchange also occurs both between an individual and other human beings and between the outer world and an individual's inner life.

When the basic tools of the **straight line** and the **curved line** are used, the form and style of

a costume can express the **emotions** of a character. Straight lines and shapes point to a character's clarity and equilibrium; they can also indicate antipathy, coldness and lack of feeling. A shirt, blouse or jacket buttoned to the neck gives the impression of a character that needs to be neat and tidy or that has withdrawn from the world. Curves convey a softness, warmth and sympathy but can also point to a bullish and overbearing nature. As soon as the shirt, blouse or jacket is unbuttoned, the character's openness and interest in others begin to speak, but the possibly unkempt appearance can also indicates muddle-headedness or carelessness.

The costume design for the central part of the body can either unite or separate the head from the limbs. A belt placed at the waist of a similar or contrasting shape, texture or color to the main garment can either unite or divide the character's appearance. Elaborate embroidery,

Intellect

Purpose

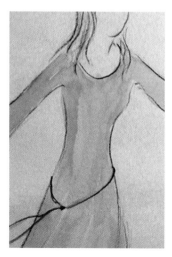

Emotion

beading and other decoration can also disguise what lives in the character's heart. A belted, buttoned and high-collared tunic can express the self-obsession of *King Lear*'s Edmund. In *Hamlet*, a tightly-buckled bodice, constricting the movement of Gertrude's diaphragm, can make her self-centeredness visible. When the costume is to unite all three parts, a smooth flow of fabric covering the whole body and with little ornamentation can help the audience to directly perceive the inner qualities of the character. In *King Lear*, a smooth, simple dress fitted to Cordelia's slender form can make her openness a visual experience. A soft, unformed shift hanging freely from the shoulders can express Ophelia's vulnerability and immaturity.

5. SYMMETRY

A general symmetry exists between the left and right sides of the body, but this principle does not apply to its front and back or its lower and upper halves. When emphasized, the symmetry of left and right can reveal uprightness and nobility. The absence of symmetry can suggest one-sidedness, even dishonesty. In the absence of symmetry in the body of Richard, Duke of Gloucester, clearly evident in his back that has a one-sided hump, Shakespeare has indicated his moral ambiguity.

Finally, the designer will need to take into consideration both the physical comfort and the level of confidence of the actors in the production: Does the actor prefer a tight or loose garment? Does the actor have a sensitive skin? What feel can give the actor most confidence when wearing the costume?

ARCHITECTURE & SET

The following principles can inform the choice of style for the set.

1. POLARITY

In the ongoing search for perfection in form, styles in architecture have alternated between clean simplicity and elaborate detail, each era using the experiences of its predecessors to create its own style. The desire to create buildings that honored the religious life on the one hand and that needed to satisfy material needs on the other were what determined each particular style. As with dress, another creative tension exists between the styles designed for purpose-built public spaces and buildings and individual tastes that are expressed in private homes. Johannes Kepler's (1571–1630) *Harmonice Mundi* indicates one of the first tools that can be used to express polarities: "The world of Lines is as eternal as the Spirit of God... the line presented him with archetypal pictures for the artistic edifice of this world... In the beginning God chose straightness and roundness in order to endow the world with the signature of the Divine."

Straightness has clarity, direction and purpose and leads to an experience of uprightness. If the set of Duke Vincentio's palace in *Measure for Measure* is created with straight lines, it will acquire the nobility that helps him to put right the state affairs that are in disarray. It may also express hardness. When put together, straight-lined shapes create sharp angles that in turn

produce a jagged appearance when lit from few lamps. Straight-lined shapes around Dionyza in *Pericles* can heighten the audience's sense of her villainy in the moment when she is planning to murder Marina.

Roundness has flexibility, gentleness, warmth and softness; it may also express weakness. When put together, rounded shapes create an impression of harmony. An excess of rounded forms can convey the atmosphere of comedy or farce. If the drinking parlor in *Twelfth Night* in which Sir Toby Belch plots to ridicule Malvolio is full of rounded forms, it can underline the comic excesses of the situation.

The **vertical** increases the height of the space and draws the eye upwards, creating a formal atmosphere. The **horizontal** widens the space and allows the gaze to wander from side to side, creating an atmosphere of ease and comfort.

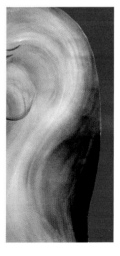

When the vertical and horizontal meet in the **diagonal**, a living relationship is created between the two spatial directions.

The space at the front of the stage has an atmosphere of intimacy and subjectivity. The back is distant and more objective. The distance and objectivity may be enhanced or exaggerated by making furniture or other items that stand close to the front of the stage larger than those positioned at the back.

The polarity of indoor and outdoor, of urban and country, is also one of the greatest contrasts to be found in a stage setting, and straight and curved lines and shapes can effectively convey the differences. In an outdoor setting, with curving branches of trees and other plants, the rounded or curved shapes create a natural country look. In an indoor setting, a curved shape lends an atmosphere of coziness or chaos; when combined with soft surfaces, rounded shapes lend warmth. Straight shapes create an impression of a city setting, with straight-edged buildings and streets. In an indoor setting the straight shapes evoke order or austerity; straight forms with hard and shiny surfaces bring a cool quality to the setting.

2. THE GOLDEN SECTION

When harmony and balance are required in the design of the stage set, the proportions of the Golden Section can be applied and may be incorporated at the same time as other, distorting elements. This apparently contradictory combination can set up dramatic tension. The opening of *Macbeth* takes place on a heath, in itself a balanced and harmonious natural setting, but when three witches appear the harmony vanishes. The drugged and unclear state of mind of *Cymbeline*'s ruling king may suggest a setting that combines balanced and distorted proportions to express the ambiguity and tensions within the character; this same quality will also be present throughout the royal household.

3. THE HOUSE

The set can be seen as the 'house' of the production and has three main elements: A house needs foundations firmly anchored in the earth on which to build the **floor**. A house also has a covering **roof**, which can also be seen as a microcosmic image of the dome of the heavens above. (Most stage designs do not usually include a roof, but leave the upper space open to accommodate the lighting and make the world of inspiration accessible.) The **walls** as the third element in the house hold the lower and the upper parts in their rightful positions

The Golden Section

and create the space between. They separate and protect the inner from the outer space. As soon as doors and windows are inserted into the walls and open and close, the relationship between inside and outside comes alive.

The three elements are connected or correspond to both the three parts of the body and to the varying inner dynamics of the production. When the ceiling or roof is lofty and vaulted, the actors' intellect or thinking has the potential to be free and clear, and the head will feel free. When the ceiling or roof is low, the actors' mental activity may stay limited to the practical and everyday, and the head may appear oppressed. A wide, open floor allows for free movement of the actors' limbs and expression of the characters' will. Rostra, steps or other pieces of set on the floor restrict the freedom of the limbs and hamper the will. The space created by the walls becomes the home of the journey of the characters' emotions just as the trunk of an actor's body houses the heart. The number, proportions and positions of doors and windows affect the characters and their interactions with others. Many windows and doors break up the uniformity of the walls and open up a vista, but they can also evoke an atmosphere of restlessness or transience.

4. SYMMETRY

The vertical axis creates symmetry between left and right and runs from the front to the back of the stage. When it is incorporated into the set design, symmetry evokes an impression of the formal and the ordered and creates a space in which reason dominates and emotions are calmed or suppressed. This symmetry can be used for formal gardens, ballrooms, courts of law and churches. It can heighten the restrained formality of Hermione's trial in *The Winter's Tale*. If the symmetry is removed, the space becomes more neutral. The joyful shepherds' feast to celebrate the end of the sheep-shearing in *The Winter's Tale* offers an opportunity to create asymmetrical set forms.

LIGHTING

The principles that apply to costume and set can also be applied to lighting.

1. POLARITY

The use of single or multiple lighting instruments creates contrasting qualities in the stage space. A group of lights used over the whole of the stage creates a wide, open space. Such a space may be what is required for the final gathering of all characters in *The Tempest*. A single lighting instrument can isolate an area of the stage, making this style of lighting useful for monologues. One spotlight used on Hamlet during his solitary reflections can emphasize his isolation. One light setting or cue can be changed to the next in two main contrasting

ways. Fast or abrupt changes make the audience aware of the lighting. If the change is slow or gradual, the mood or quality of both light settings prevails, and the audience will not notice any changes.

2. THE SPACE

Lighting the entire stage in the same way creates a harmonious and balanced atmosphere that may also make the audience a little dreamy. Lighting the different areas of the stage in contrasting ways creates definition and depth in each of the areas and heightens the audience's awareness of their different qualities. If the light in the upper area of the stage space is emphasized over the middle and lower zones, the space appears to be light and airy. If the lighting in the lower area is stronger than elsewhere, the darkness above can make it appear heavy and oppressive.

3. SYMMETRY

The vertical axis can be used in the lighting design to create symmetry that runs from front to back between the left and the right sides of the stage space. When the lighting is equally balanced on both sides of the stage, it allows the audience to focus on the central area. When

one side is lit in a different way than the other, all kinds of alternative situations can be created that express the varying inner quality of any particular moment.

FINAL THOUGHTS

Working with the principles that determine the style and form for any aspect of stage design can sometimes feel limiting, and this can lead to questions: Is what has been described in this chapter necessary to create a good design? Can the designer not put his trust in his own creative resources alone? When the designer aims to both serve the essential idea of the production and support the actors in their own creative process, the choices made ultimately become an integral part of the design, whether they address style and form, texture or color. So if the design is started from this perspective, the principles are less likely to block the designer's creativity.

What can also help to deal with any sense of limitation is the designer's making the imagination the principal tool with which to find the colors, textures, style and form. Then any guidelines are more likely to be experienced as catalysts rather than obstacles to the designer's creativity.

HAMLET: Design sketch for Battlements scene

Design sketch for Players scene

V
COSTUME

"Thou villain base, know'st me not by my clothes?"

"No, nor thy tailor, ...which, as it seems, make thee."

Cymbeline, Act IV, scene 2

I once saw a production of Goethe's *Faust*, in the opening scene of which Faust speaks of his inner struggles with his studies. Although the actor playing the part was moving to watch, he was wearing a cloak made of stiff, bulky linen that refused to drape, so that his long cuffs were stiff and stuck out. The consequence of this was that, while the character was pondering his deepest problems, the cuffs of the cloak were busy reaching out to the audience. I found it difficult to concentrate on the content of his words and wondered instead what the intention behind this was and whether the designer was aware of its effect.

I realized from this experience that we only notice a costume when it appears at odds with the character or story, and I decided to pay more attention to the details of the garments actors were dressed in to help them bring their characters to life. I began to take a great interest in the exact cuts of garments in general and to observe how each cut affected me: What part of the body did it emphasize and how? The shape of a costume or of part of it can, of course, either be in harmony with the other parts or with the other costumes on the stage or not, but whatever the choice, it should be made consciously.

Costumes have always influenced the way in which the human body moves, and when fashions change, the overall shape of the body and the way it is carried gradually changes with them. For example, crinolines or panniers, the wide-hooped petticoats that filled out a lady's skirt at the sides and back in the eighteenth century, brought delicacy to the upper body and a gliding effect to the walk, while bustles, which extended only the back of the skirt, emphasized the uprightness of the wearer and made each step look precise. In a similar way, the doublet and hose that came into fashion for men in the sixteenth century brought about a number of changes: They lengthened the upper body, pushed back the shoulders, widened the hips and emphasized the shapeliness of the legs, and so a brand new elegant pose came about that allowed for a swagger in the walk. The following descriptions of individual items of clothing illustrate how different elements of a costume can help to transform the actor into the character by highlighting one particular part of the body over another and in this way give visible expression to the character's individual qualities, both physical and psychological, and enhance the actor's characterization.

CLOTHING THE HEAD & NECK

At the top of the human form, what may first catch our attention are the face and head, with the accompanying transformative hairstyles, wigs, hats and headdresses. These can all express different aspects of the character's thinking.

1. HAIR & WIGS

As the head's natural headdress, **hair** can be styled in many ways that draw either more or less attention to it. Pulling the hair away from the face, for example, can emphasize its classical beauty or severity and plainness, while if a young girl's long hair is dressed with ringlets or curls that are draped around the face, the character will acquire a lightness and playfulness. By altering the actor's facial hair for a male character, by adding a false beard and/or a moustache, a marked change can be made to the maturity and dignity of the character. If either is shaved off, the actor will look younger and more naïve. A **wig** can enhance the character more strongly still, because it alters the face more than any change to the hair, and, if the play specifies that the character must have a specific hair color, using a wig is often the simplest way to bring about that change.

2. HEADDRESSES & HATS

For the character whose main activity is to reflect and perhaps ponder on single thoughts, such as on the meaning of life, for longer periods of time, whatever covers the head, home of the thinking, can be modest and discreet, in plain color and simple fabric and style. For a dandy-like character, on the other hand, who tends to entertain rapidly-changing, frivolous or

selfish thoughts, a frivolous play of fabrics on the head in a style created just for him and that attracts the audience's attention can make his whimsical nature more believable. Clowns are often the sharpest wits in a play and need a headdress or hat that stands out above the other characters'. One with sharp lines and angles will emphasize the sharpness of his wit; rounded ones will render his humor less aggressive. A head-scarf or shawl tied closely around the head can express that the character has no interest in or time for vanity, especially if he or she comes from impoverished circumstances.

3. COLLARS & NECKLINES

The type of neckline and collar on the costume either allows the spectator to overlook the neck

and throat or draws the eye to them. This part of the body is the home of the larynx, the organ that enables speech, and as most garments need an opening at the neck, the position and size of the fastening may relate to the manner of the character's speech, either by contradicting

« *MERCHANT OF VENICE: Jessica*

or harmonizing with it. In Edwardian times, for example, when conventional etiquette did not welcome plain speaking, high collars that buttoned tightly at the throat were high fashion. At the time of the Inquisition in Spain, large white stiff ruffs were worn at the neck above dark jackets, creating the impression that their purpose was to prevent the character's possibly dogmatic thoughts from being influenced by any such personal feelings as compassion. The open-throated shirt suits characters with big hearts and open minds such as sailors and others whom life has taught to be generous and easy-going. The wide, low necklines in women's clothing fashionable in the seventeenth century that exposed the neck and throat can make visible that the character takes pleasure in speaking and loves gossip, while for elderly characters that want to appear more restrained, the neck may be covered by placing a shawl around the shoulders that can then be wrapped round the throat, as if sealing the lips and prohibiting the expression of personal feelings.

CLOTHING THE WHOLE BODY

1. GOWNS & DRESSES

Garments that clothe the trunk and lower limbs in their entirety can convey a sense of the overall personality of the character to the audience. They create an impression of unity or harmony in the character and give their wearers the sensation that they are more upright and dignified than otherwise. If the gown or dress is cut with a long vertical line at its center, this may

heighten the impression of the character's wisdom and integrity, and he or she will appear to be well-'centered.' When this same line is moved to one side, and the audience's eye moves with it, it appears to hinder or pervert the character's striving for wisdom. If a belt is added, it will detract from the unified impression that the gown or dress creates unless made of similar cloth to the garment. If the character has a large, round belly, and if any belt used is hung low, the same gown or dress can create the impression of pompousness. The longer the gown, the greater the age of the character, whereas a short tunic can indicate that the character is young and perhaps naïve. However, a gown alone, without a cloak or coat, often makes the wearer look only half-dressed; this effect can be used if the character is caught out or wants to appear unprepared for what is to come.

2. COATS & CLOAKS

There are many styles of cloak or coat that lend themselves to highlighting a character's personality. They can hang from one or both shoulders, be cut long or short and have sleeves or not. A full drape of fabric cut at hip-length for a man and gathered into generous folds at the collar that swing easily when the character moves creates a lively impression, as if he is ready to leap into action at a moment's notice. A cloak or coat with fabric gathered at some odd places and on others left flat and smooth, perhaps with an uneven hemline and so appearing tangled and disordered to the audience might well suit a confused character. A cloak or coat with long, drooping lines made of a limp fabric that makes it look weighty even if the fabric is thin may indicate that the character is weak-willed or ineffective. A smooth, well-shaped and well-proportioned garment can indicate that the character's life is well-ordered. Add decoration to any part of the cloak to enhance specific qualities.

CLOTHING
THE UPPER BODY

1. BODICES & JACKETS

Bodices and jackets clothe the ribcage, the home of the heart and lungs and also of human feelings and inner life in general. As the qualities of a character's soul are perhaps the most important element of any role, that not only the character's words can convey, the specific details of the bodice or jacket can contribute to the revelation of the character's inner nature with considerable subtlety. Tight-fitting bodices and jackets can convey alertness or wakefulness in a character; if taken to an extreme, they make a character look brittle. Flowing robes

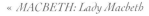
« MACBETH: Lady Macbeth

convey dreaminess; if the actor's body underneath is slender, the consequence may be that the character appears fragile. The same effect can be achieved by highlighting the waistline, which will also draw attention to the character's slenderness. A blousy, loose jacket or bodice made in a heavy fabric can imply a heaviness or drowsiness in a character; the same shape in rougher fabric may well be a suitable costume for a bully.

2. SLEEVES & CUFFS

The arms are usually continually active and making gestures when actors speak, so the cloth that covers them can exaggerate those movements and enhance their expressiveness. A generous and expansive character needs wide

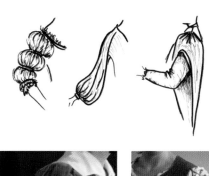

sleeves, possibly made of a soft fabric, for a quick gesture may be lost in wide, loose sleeves, which better accommodate slower, fuller movements and lend maturity to the wearer. A narrow sleeve made of a stiff, unbending cloth may hint at a tight-fisted and mean character. The

MEASURE FOR MEASURE: Mariana

top of the sleeve can create a wide or narrow shoulder. The well-known figure of King Henry VIII is a good example of how padded sleeves that are widest at the top can make for an imposing width at the shoulders. His tailors must have used large quantities of buckram to make this possible. A tight cuff at the wrist can indicate a nimble alertness, and any decoration at the cuffs will draw attention to the hands, especially if the actor wears rings.

3. BELTS

The horizontal line of a belt cuts the body in half and can therefore take attention away from other parts of the body, so it is advisable to use belts with restraint. But they can also help to define the overall shape of the body. Waistlines have risen and fallen as styles have changed through the ages and influenced how the body moves. For example, the low, loose girdles draped over the hips of ladies in the Middle Ages created a graceful, relaxed pose, which became an expression of a calm, unruffled nature. The Empire line of the nineteenth century, on the other hand, placed the belt at the other extreme, directly below the bust, and drew the wearer's weight onto the front of the foot; this can express a nervous disposition. Between the two positions is the body's natural waist, the most suitable place for a belt for characters that have a balanced nature. A tight belt can indicate neatness and orderliness, while a loose one may convey the opposite. Finally, wherever the belt is on the body, it should not be so tight that it hinders the full movement of the diaphragm and restricts proper breathing.

CLOTHING THE LOWER BODY

1. SKIRTS & TROUSERS

The lower half of the body and the way human beings walk and stand reveal how we are connected with the ground beneath us. Young children may walk on tiptoes at first before they feel grounded enough to walk with their heels

as well. When a skirt or pair of trousers in a heavy cloth covers the legs, it can slow down the walk and highlight the character's earthiness. Characters with their head in the clouds, and therefore little or no relationship to the earth, may wear a skirt or trousers made of a flimsy fabric and so be able to move with greater speed and lightness. A tightly-fitting skirt or pair of trousers highlights the shape of the body, restricts movement and, as a conse-

« Mock crinolin

quence, can evoke an impression of strong self-awareness or haughtiness. Wide skirts or trousers allow for fast-moving action, and tights or stockings offer the greatest freedom of movement. Both allow characters to focus on matters beyond themselves when necessary.

2. UNDERGARMENTS & LININGS

By definition all 'under'-garments are worn beneath 'over'-clothes and intended not to be visible to anyone but the wearer. But when shirts and blouses (not underwear, strictly speaking), petticoats and bloomers peep out from underneath a top layer of a costume, their whiteness or general contrast to the over-garment can give the whole outfit a freshness and sparkle. They will also reveal that there is more to the character than what is seen on the surface. Only a small corner of any piece of underwear, just briefly glimpsed when the character is moving, betrays that he or she has a hidden side. This glimpse tantalizes the audience and can point to a cheekiness or slyness in the character; it can also reveal the true colors of an otherwise well disguised villain. The lining of an outer garment can also have this effect and can be a useful tool in alerting the audience that there is another, possibly quite opposing drive or quality in the character.

3. SHOES & BOOTS

Footwear is the one part of the costume design where the actor's comfort and security have priority over the artistic. However, the feet need to be part of the whole costume and to give the actor, whether playing an old man or a

young girl, a soldier or a dancer, the possibility to move in character. A heavy boot will create a weighty, masculine tread and heighten the sense of the character's seriousness. A sandal will show off the lower leg to its full advantage and its lightness imbue the wearer with lightness. A light, soft slipper with a heel will ensure the actor walks with a feminine step. A jewel or decoration attached to the slipper will draw the audience's attention to the daintiness of the foot.

ACCESSORIES

4. JEWELRY

A piece of jewelry draws the eye immediately to a specific part of the body, such as the head (crowns or tiaras and bejeweled hats), the neck (necklaces), the bustline, natural waist or hips (ornamented belts), the wrists (bracelets) and hands (rings) or the feet (shoe buckles). A piece of jewelry can add a finishing touch to an elegantly dressed character of aristocratic or wealthy origins. The jewel's sparkle can be an asset to a character, but it can be distracting on stage if it continually catches the light, so needs to be used sparingly to retain its effectiveness. A small dab of grease will soften the effect.

5. ARMOR

Armor is designed to protect the wearer against attack, creating an impregnable and often cumbersome hard metal covering of part or all of the body. Whether a character has only one piece of armor, such as a helmet, breastplate or shield, or wears an entire suit, the metallic sheen of its surface when under lighting can lift a dark and chaotic mood of conflict and transform it into something that can inspire the courage for battle. Armor makes the wearer more upright and immediately highlights his heroic stature.

6. DECORATION

After every aspect of the costume has been finished, decoration can add final highlights, often quite quickly, to specific areas of any costume. Patterns embroidered or painted on and around the neckline enhance the upper body. Embroidered cuffs bring focus to the hand movements. A beaded belt emphasizes the waist. An elaborate border on the hem can give weight to the whole appearance of the character.

FINAL THOUGHTS

Any or all of the details described here may be worked into any costume style or period. It is just important to be selective about what elements are incorporated into the design of any one costume. The overall aim when designing the costume should be to bring focus to the most prominent feature of the character and to allow the rest of the costume to blend into the overall appearance of the play. If designer and actor come to a mutual understanding of who the character is, and the designer creates a costume that is capable of conveying this to the audience, both physically and psychologically, then both actor and production have been immensely helped. It is vital that the design support the actor in every detail and is never in competition with those who embody the characters.

VI
MAKEUP, MASK & PUPPETRY

"God hath given you one face,

and you make yourselves another."

Hamlet, Act III, scene 1

On our way to the United States some years ago, one of the airport check-in staff took one look at my hand luggage and said: "That goes into the hold!" I replied that it was too fragile for that, and unzipped the lid to show her my solitary marionette, Max, hanging on his peg. She stared at the puppet, and the severe expression on her face vanished. Without taking her eyes off Max, she asked my husband whether he could put on a tie. Once the tie was in place and, without uttering a single word about Max, she upgraded us to business class. When I later took him through security and he appeared on the screen of the x-ray machine, several officials gathered around, curious to see him in the flesh, so I opened the lid again, briefly moved him, and they began to smile. At check-in on the return journey, Max worked his wonders again on the American staff member and she, too, upgraded us.

What do spectators see when watching a mask or puppet in play? How can faces that do not move and have no life of their own potentially awaken such a wide range of emotions in any-one watching them? A look at the role and nature of the human face may begin to explain this.

During a performance the audience's attention may wander from one part of an actor's body to another, depending on what the actor is doing. If he or she is listening at the side or back of the stage, the audience is more likely to take in the entire figure. If the performer is active at the center or front, the audience absorbs primarily the movements of the body, but if he or she is speaking and standing still at the same time, then the face will be the part of the body that the audience watches.

If the designer is working with the principles set out so far, he or she will see the face as an extension of the body and as part of the whole human being, and consequently makeup becomes as much a part of the transformation of the actor into the character as the hat or shoes of the costume.

I am aware that this approach may not be in step with a lot of contemporary practice, which uses no or very little makeup and, when it is applied, primarily serves the definition of the actor's personal features. However, modifying the features to create the character does not necessarily involve the application of layers of heavy foundation and intense colors. Indeed, here less is probably more.

Max

THE FACE

The following points that belong to the essential nature of the face have their implications for makeup, the mask and the puppet face when a specific aspect of character needs to be highlighted.

1. METAMORPHOSIS

During a lifetime the face is in a continual process of change. The child is filled with energy from within, and the skin is full and smooth and has a rosy glow; the wrinkled features of elderly people are perhaps what their life experiences have imprinted on their faces. In the ages between childhood and old age, the face is a visible statement of the evolving character and comes to express more and more of the human individuality.

2. GENERAL FEATURES

The whole face occupies the front of the head and is usually framed by hair. The uppermost part, the **forehead** is part of the curved dome of the head that mirrors in miniature the roof of **the heavens**. The **cheeks** and the **nose** slanting downwards form the middle area; breathing and taking in the scents and smells of the surrounding **air** or **atmosphere** are their main activities. The **jaw**, including the chin, forms the base of the face; it is its most mobile element or 'limb' that when chewing breaks down the food grown in **the earth**. The face can be understood and seen as an echo or mirror image of the diverse aspects of the world around it.

3. CORRESPONDENCES

These three realms of the face—above, below and the area between—also have their correspondences in and connections to the three parts of the human body as described in the last two chapters, The **jaw** relates to the lower limbs, the **forehead** to the head as a whole and the **cheeks** and **nose** to the chest, heart and lungs. An instance of when this connection is clearly visible is when the legs or hands are particularly active; that is the moment when the jaw often juts forward.

4. INNER QUALITIES

The unique forms of the three main parts of the face, and the specific relationship between them, may also express the inner qualities of its owner, revealing his or her strengths and weaknesses. A high, domed **forehead** may point to a capacity for clear and profound thinking and be seen in a person of powerful intellect. A strong **jaw** may indicate a dominant will, as a craftsperson or laborer may have. The **cheeks** and **nose** are linked to the realm of emotions and feelings and may show the highs and lows of

photo by Karen Rees

the dynamic relationship between the self and the world. Such a person in whom these are strong features may be an artist or a caregiver, in whom sensitivity is the predominant characteristic.

5. TRANSITIONS

The **mouth**, situated between the lower and the middle regions of the face, makes it possible for us to take food into the body and to breathe and speak, an activity that uses audible words to send thoughts and feelings into the world. The direction of activity or movement, from inside to outside, involved in speaking is the opposite of the outside to inside direction of movement of eating, and the shape of the two lips indicates their dual purpose; while the corners of the mouth turn inward, the skin inside the mouth turns outward to form the upper and lower lips.

The **eyes** are between the middle and upper regions of the face and are linked to the air and the heavens. They look out into the objectivity of the physical world; they also gaze inward and reflect, and so are part of the human soul. Here, too, there is a polarity of direction, and the form of the eyes echoes their dual purpose; the lens enables the eye to focus on outer objects and the retina reflects.

The **ears**, on either side of the middle of the face, make it possible for us to hear. The forms that echo this purpose are hidden inside the head, but the visible shapes repeat in miniature the forms of the entire face: the upper curve echoes the dome of the head, the lower lobe

the mobility of the jaw and between these the intricate curves that echo the undulations of the cheeks and nose. They in turn link the top and the bottom of the face.

The **neck**, which both holds the face and head in place above the shoulders and then links them to the rest of the body does not emerge as a form until the child begins to stand and then walk.

MAKEUP

Makeup transforms the actor's face into the character he or she will portray. It both softens and dulls the overall natural sheen of the skin

and enlarges and defines the individual features to make them visible to the audience.

1. SKIN TONE

The shading of various areas of the face in a variety of colors is a first, more general stage of transformation that can change the character's age, state of health and reveal the temperament.

Age: Firstly, makeup can both reveal and then alter the age of the character. At the beginning of *The Winter's Tale*, Hermione appears as a young and happy queen and mother, and the actor's face can be made up with ivory and rose-red tones that are softly blended. After sixteen years of suffering, Hermione's features will

have changed, and in order to make the changes visible, the tone of the base color can become paler and her cheeks hollow by applying a deeper brown-red color below the cheekbones.

Health: Both the color of the complexion and the toning of the skin illustrate the general state of health. The tone of the base can be varied to make that of a particular character's visible. A healthy constitution, such as *Twelfth Night*'s Sir Toby Belch, needs warm colors. An ailing character needs to use cooler tones, including yellows and greens. Sir Andrew Aguecheek's name in the same play already indicates the pale tone of his skin.

Personality: The skin tone may also illustrate the **temperament** of a character. In *As You Like*

It, Jaques' **melancholia** may be visible in a sallow tone and darker shading under the eyes and cheekbones. The **choleric** Paulina in *The Winter's Tale* can be given a ruddy complexion and rounded highlights on the cheeks. From the same play, a light and fresh pink skin tone and bright nose can demonstrate Autolycus' **sanguine** and curious nature. A warm but pale skin tone and undefined features may make visible the slow and **phlegmatic** temperament of Launcelot Gobbo in *The Merchant of Venice*.

2. FACIAL CONTOURS

Lines added to the basic tones can individualize the features of the character's face. They may be used to reveal a character's strengths or weaknesses by emphasizing one area of the face and understating another.

3. FOREHEAD

As an illustration of an intelligent mind, a high forehead can be achieved by either pulling the hair back firmly or removing the hair that grows below the line required. Vincentio's perceptive intelligence of the needs of his people in *Measure for Measure* may justify creating a high forehead. If the hair is combed forward, the height of the forehead can be reduced, thus giving the impression of a simpler mind. The clown in *The Winter's Tale*, not renowned for his intelligence, may benefit from a low forehead, which can be achieved by having his hair plastered to his brow. A character that focuses on the everyday struggles of material existence may be given vertical creases between the eyes to illustrate continual frowning.

In *The Merchant of Venice* Shylock's obsession with his money exemplifies this. When awe and wonder at all that life and the beyond offer live strongly in a character, this may be made visible by drawing horizontal lines across the brow. This is a strong feature of Prospero, in *The Tempest*, whose knowledge and wisdom can command the supernatural world.

4. EYEBROWS

The lines above the eyes created by tiny hairs may be thick and bushy and thus prominent, or pale, fine and almost invisible. They may also have many varied shapes and positions on the forehead. They can strongly express aspects of both the personality in general and also the character's reaction to changing situations. If the actor's eyebrows do not have the shape and position needed, they can be covered with the base tone and then new ones created in any shape, width, position and color. When eyebrows slant up and outwards, they make a self-centered and opportunistic impression, which may be useful for Lady Macbeth. When they slant gently downwards, they convey an inwardness and profundity, which can highlight the philosopher in Jaques in *As You Like It*. If they are more strongly slanted, the character looks like a simpleton. Bushy and low eyebrows in a more or less straight line—this may be further accentuated by the use of false hair—illustrate low-leveled motives, such as those of Sir Toby Belch. Fine and delicately curved eyebrows may express Miranda's high-minded and pure intentions in *The Tempest*.

5. EYES

The shape of the eye may be emphasized by applying a dark outline. A sharp-eyed look is created if the outer corners are lifted, as may emphasize the trickster in Autolycus in *The Winter's Tale*. The Queen in *Cymbeline* may also have high outer corners, but a darkening of the inner corners may lend a mean, half-closed expression that disguises her evil intentions. Bringing the outer corners down creates a sorrowful or anxious expression, such as Ophelia may have when distressed by Hamlet's harsh words. Hamlet's eyes may have a less prominent outline, to give more weight to his many inward-looking moments.

6. NOSE

The nose can be evidence of the racial origin of an individual more than any other part of the face. To create a flat, short and broad nose for the Moor Othello, for example, the highlight across the bridge of the nose, including the flared nostrils, may be wide and blended gently into the base tone of the cheeks. To create a long, curved and slender nose, such as may be given to the Jewish Venetian merchant Shylock, the highlight on the bridge may be narrow with darker sides. If the highlight on the bridge of the nose is shortened, the character may look younger. When the same highlight is lengthened, the character appears to be older. The tip of the nose can be reddened when the character is known to be a regular and excessive drinker, such as Stephano in *The Tempest*.

7. CHEEKS

The cheekbones and soft flesh below them on either side of the nose can be highlighted and shadowed to indicate the age of the character. High and soft cheekbones make a character younger. Lower, lined cheekbones increase the age. Highlighting the cheekbones and darkening the area below gives a thin and highly-strung impression, such as might suit Lady Macbeth. To give the impression of a more easy-going and older character, the emphasis can be brought lower and made to look fuller by highlighting the jawline, such as the Earl of Gloucester may have at the opening of *King Lear*. To create an angry look, as may characterize the face of Edmund in the same play, the lines either side of the nose that reach down to the mouth can be darkened.

8. MOUTH

Just as the eyebrows can be completely transformed, the edges of the actor's lips can be covered with the base color to wipe away the actor's mouth shape, and the character's individual mouth can then be built up on this blank canvas. The transformation of the mouth is pronounced in the traditional makeup of a Geisha, over whose personal mouth shape the lips are painted in a tiny, heart-shaped form. The circus clown exaggerates the size of his mouth. For a more natural look, the size of the mouth can be changed more subtly by darkening the outline of the mouth along the edges of the lips. When the dark line is brought in to reduce the size of the lip surface, so that less lip is visible, the character's appearance becomes mean and pinched. Such a lip form may be given to Dionyza in *Pericles* to express her jealousy. If a dark line is drawn outside the edges of the lips, so that they appear fuller and wider, the character appears to be more generous. The fun-loving Benedick in *Much Ado about Nothing* is perhaps a good example.

9. CHIN

The chin completes the image of the face. This too can be blended into the neck by the base tone or highlighted with a paler tone. A strong and forceful individual such as the same Benedick may have a jutting chin to emphasize his strength. To do this, the center of the chin and the jawline can be highlighted with a light base tone and the neck darkened. A lily-livered character such as *Twelfth Night*'s Sir Andrew may need to have the contours of his chin toned down by leaving the base tone on both chin and neck untouched by color.

10. EARS

Both hair and hats often hide the ears, but they still need to be included in the general base tone covering. Ears that lie flat against the head give an impression of elegance, whereas ones that stand out from the side of the head may create a comical look. Highlighting the outer edges of the ears can emphasize the character's love of eavesdropping. Polonius in *Hamlet* is a prime example, as he has a long-standing habit of listening to private conversations.

THE MASK

The mask requires a stronger imaginative engagement of the audience than the mobile human face with makeup. At the same time it extends and heightens the possibilities of makeup. Masks are created by covering part or all of the face with a hardened substance that is given a shape that enhances or emphasizes the character's features. The more the face is covered, the less it is possible for the actor to rely on his or her facial expressions, and so the movements of the whole body must tell the story.

1. PART, HALF & THREE-QUARTER MASKS

These lend themselves to the exaggeration of a particular feature, especially for caricature or disguise. It allows the actor to speak and be heard clearly but adds a fixed appearance to the

Carneval mask

masked part of the face. This presents actors with a new range of challenges, as they discover how to blend with or integrate into the mask the changing facial expressions of those parts of the face still visible to the audience.

2. FULL MASKS

These hide the actor's features completely and fix the whole facial appearance into that of the character. The full mask may seem mysterious to the audience and when a number of them are used at the same time may initially create some anxiety in the spectator. But ultimately they draw the audience in and make them want to know what lives inside them. They also invite them to look more attentively. The full mask freezes the face into one expression that alters only with the help of the imagination and inner participation of the viewer. It is remarkable how often the audience experiences changing and varied emotions in the fixed features of the full mask.

The fully masked actor obviously works without speaking because the mouth is covered, and so performing with full masks means that the actor needs to give much greater attention to creating an active inner process. A performer must be able to radiate his or her character's inner life to the audience through movements, so that they can experience what the character is inwardly experiencing. The fact is that the less we speak, the stronger our inner awareness or inner life becomes, and it is essential that the actor wearing a mask is aware of this. This continual stream of inner activity is what gives the character life and connects the actor and the audience.

3. ANIMAL & OBJECT MASKS

When designing masks that bear no resemblance to the human face, the actor's face can either remain unseen or be shown within or beneath the mask. The second option honors and respects the humanity in the facial form and enables the audience to see the actor's changing expressions. The mask can be placed on top of the actor's head and the makeup and the painted mask blended. When the animal or object mask is to cover the entire face and head, it may be made of transparent fabric built on a wire frame so that the face remains partially visible. An example of such an animal mask is the ass's head given to Bottom in *A Midsummer Night's Dream*. Here it may be important to have the face partially visible because Bottom himself does not know that his appearance has changed.

4. MASKS AS PROPS

Not all masks convey aspects of the character; their purpose may rather be to hide the face temporarily. Such masks can be made as props by fitting them onto long rods or sticks. This kind of mask lends itself well to carnival and, for example, to the masked ball in *Much Ado about Nothing*, in which the characters can say much they would not say if their identities were known to the listeners.

5. DESIGNING MASKS

Giving an actor a mask for the character means that the character's face can be integrated more effectively into the entire design of costume and set than when applying makeup only. The close collaborations between both designer and director and between designer and mask-wearer are therefore more essential in this realm of stage design than in any other. In fact, the actor may need help in learning how to work with a mask, and then a neutral mask, free of any distinctive features, character or coloring, can help performers to familiarize themselves with the new ways of moving.

6. COLOR & TEXTURE

Both the mask's base coloring and painted features again offer opportunities for unlimited and fantastic exaggeration, and the same principles of coloring that work for makeup also apply here. But the color of the mask responds to the lighting in the same way as the fabric of the costume or scenery and not as makeup does, and lighting may or may not influence the overall expression on the mask's surface. When the mask is smooth and relatively flat, the lighting does not change its general appearance. If the mask has a rough or a strongly contoured surface, any changes in lighting alter its expression.

7. FORM & PROPORTIONS

When designing a mask, the designer need not be restricted to realistic or naturalistic imagery. Indeed, the fantastic may be the strongest inspiration, and the production using fantastic masks may well engage the audience's imagination in a more powerful way than if the masks are realistic. The mask's size and shape need have no boundaries, and a set of proportions may be created free of any conventions. However, the exaggeration of any one feature will remain as the one expression throughout the performance, and it is also important to consider the character's development through the play. An **over-sized** mask can make the body look top-heavy and the character clumsy. An **under-sized** mask enlarges the body in proportion and the character becomes pompous and overbearing. A **round and curved** mask makes the body plump and the character generous. A **square and sharp-angled mask** makes the body thin and the character mean and hard. An **over-wide** mask makes the face expansive and the character extrovert. An **over-long** mask makes the face reflective and the character introvert. **Big, wide-open eyes** may express surprise and wonder. **Small, half-closed eyes** may express calculation and evil intent. **Wide-set eyes** may look innocent and youthful. **Narrow-set eyes** may accentuate meanness. A **large mouth** may dominate the mask's image and make the character an incessant talker. A **small mouth** may almost disappear and express the character's reluctance to speak. However, any design of a mask must take into account the actor's ability to wear it comfortably, be able to breathe and not collide with fellow actors.

THE PUPPET

With its beginnings in ancient Asian cultures, puppet theatre preceded the beginnings of what is called theatre today, and in recent years puppets have been playing an ever greater role in contemporary theatre. So the stage designer may well be asked to include puppets in the overall design of a production.

In fact, the puppet is another step removed from the actor and a performer in its own right, with equal status, so it can become the actor's companion. It is therefore advisable to treat puppets as characters played either by a puppeteer or an actor and to give as much attention to their design as to any other aspect of the overall production, using all the principles described so far.

One thing separates the puppet from the human actor, however: There is no discrepancy between the outer and the inner in a puppet, as can be easily perceived when the puppet moves. The puppet has the ability to be entirely true to itself, to its own character and, in contrast to the actor, has no trace of a private personality. To the audience the puppet embodies a strength and purity of individuality that speaks directly to them, so they can identify with and come close to an experience of being the character. Therefore, the designer needs to step into the character and identify with it, too, in order to create the features, body and costume of a puppet that express this individuality as convincingly as possible.

Finally, as a sort of answer to the question asked at the beginning of this chapter, because the inner life and the outer form of the puppet are in complete harmony, it is hardly surprising that the audience experiences different inner qualities in the puppet when it adopts different outer forms or gestures. The static facial features seem to change expression and move with the emotions the puppet experiences, and whether these are strong or subtle, the viewer can be moved as much as the puppet appears to be itself. The face of a puppet and the tilt of its head when in play seem to speak directly to the heart, as though the puppet is speaking even though everyone knows that it cannot.

1. TYPES OF PUPPETS

The differences in the size, structure and appearance of the different kinds of puppets mean that each has a specific quality of expression and can play its individual role in all kinds of performances. In addition, every kind of puppet can be played with the puppeteer hidden or visible, either dressed in black so that he or she fades into the background, or dressed to blend in with or be part of the action on stage.

Finger Puppets: Finger puppets are small character or animal heads that can be fitted onto a finger. Finger puppets are most useful for close-up and children's play.

Glove Puppets: Glove puppets consist of a head, two hands and a costume fitted over the player's hand. Glove puppets can be played in a booth or freely in any environment.

Rod Puppets: Rod puppets have a head, hands and a costume of any size, all fixed to rods or poles. They are controlled either by a single player from inside for a small puppet or by several players from outside. Rod puppets can be played in a booth, on stage or in an open environment.

Glove-Rod Puppets: Although this is not a common form of puppet, the combination of glove and rod makes more differentiated movements possible. The left puppet hand has a glove fitting for the puppeteer's left middle finger. The right puppet hand is on a short rod for the puppeteer's right hand. The head is on another short rod for the puppeteer's left forefinger and thumb. The costume is a large piece of fabric with head and hands inserted. Glove-rod puppets can be played on the puppeteer's lap or in a booth.

String Puppets or Marionettes: In a marionette the head, hands and feet are connected to a flexible body and costume of any size and suspended on threads from a control. The control required to move the puppet's body and limbs can be designed in a variety of ways, and a wooden cross with a hole at each of the four ends is the simplest and most common. The head thread can be attached to the center of the cross; the hand thread can be attached to both hands through the front hole; the thread between the puppet's shoulder-blades can be attached to the back hole; the knee threads can be attached to the holes left and right. String puppets or marionettes are played on a stage or open floor.

Shadow Puppets: These are simple silhouettes of character or animal shapes that are then attached to rods. Lit from behind, they are played on the back of a screen. Shadow puppets lend themselves to any size or type of performance.

Bunraku Puppets: This is a particular type of Japanese puppet that is usually life-sized. The head, hands, feet and cloth body are controlled by several puppeteers; the master puppeteer controls the head. Bunraku puppets are usually played on a theatre stage.

Glove puppets

Rod puppet

String puppet

Shadow puppets

2. PLAYING THE PUPPET

Every three-dimensional puppet is challenging to control, by one of three types. The **finger**, **glove** and **rod puppets** are played from below, with a direct, hands-on action that makes for a direct and close relationship between the player and the puppet. The **string puppet** or **marionette** is played from above. This creates a more detached and indirect relationship, in which the player seems to take on the role of God and directs events from on high. The two-dimensional **shadow puppet** is played from behind. These three types of puppet can be used both to complement each other and to express contrasting elements or groups of characters within a play or story. In a fairy tale, for example, the less earthly figures, such as fairies, can be moved from above on strings, while the earthier characters can be glove or finger puppets moved from below; shadow puppets can be played behind the backdrop at particular moments as, for example, dream images.

3. THE PUPPET HEAD

It is generally assumed that the human head is round, but for the purposes of making puppet heads, it is more useful to imagine its three-dimensional form as closer to the shape of an egg, with the pointed end of the egg as the chin. Seen both from above and the back, in two dimensions only, the form resembles the five sides of a pentagon. If the back of the head is completely round, it can indicate intelligence. When it is flatter, the character appears more simple minded. The face occupies one sixth of the surface of the adult head. In puppetry this proportion can be changed to emphasize varying aspects of the character, and the following is an archetypal polarity: A large head and small face may indicate an introverted character; a small head and large face may indicate an extroverted character.

4. THE PUPPET FACE

The human face is more or less symmetrical between left and right, i.e., on the vertical axis, but not between above and below, i.e., on the horizontal axis. Looking at the egg-shaped form from the front, the eyes divide the face into approximately two halves and the horizontal levels of the hairline and the mouth roughly divide each half into quarters. With a puppet these proportions can be altered to emphasize specific characteristics. For the archetypal wicked stepmother in a fairy tale, the face may be narrowed and the cheeks hollowed, the eye level lowered and the eyes themselves reduced to slits, while the chin can be extended and sharpened. The archetypal fairy godmother may have a widened face with rounded cheeks, normal eye level at normal height and the eyes open, while the chin may be shortened and given a dimple. The truer to ideal human proportions the puppet face and form are, the more human it becomes, and the prince and princess, as ideal archetypes, may be given these proportions.

All my puppets have eye-hollows to enable their eyes to focus and gie more expression than solid painted eyeballs can achieve.

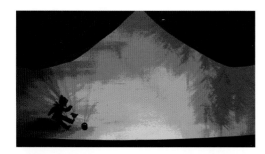

BRUNO by E. Edmunds

'Strawberry'

5. PUPPET HANDS

The movement of the hands is often an extension of the activity of speaking, and after the face, they create a second strong point of focus. They are the most mobile part of the body and can become the 'speaking voice' of the puppet, echoing the gestures the head makes to intensify their expression. The palms and fingertips of the actor's or puppeteer's hands are rounded, soft and particularly sensitive to touch, while the back of the hand is flatter, bony and hard. The many joints in the fingers give enormous flexibility, and the intricate structure of the wrist increases this. Thanks to this flexibility, an infinite variety of gestures becomes possible. A puppet with a high brow may have slender hands and long, sensitive fingers. A puppet with a heavy jowl and rounded face may have wide workman's hands with short fingers. These examples are archetypal characters: the thinker, who may use his intellect for good or evil, and the artisan or craftsman, who may be skilled or clumsy. These features can demonstrate that the hands make the character's lifestyle visible.

6. THE PUPPET BODY

The body of an actor, with or without a mask, obviously has definite form and proportions, and conventionally the designer uses the costume to help change the actor's look. In a puppet, however, the form and proportions can be varied much more strongly to express the character's inner nature. The slender and long-limbed puppet appears active, serious and sensitive. A round-shaped puppet body with short limbs seems full of humor or perhaps bossy. A shifty character may be distorted and unsymmetrical. A noble king or prince may have a well-proportioned and symmetrical body.

FINAL THOUGHTS

Thanks to continual technological developments, new forms of puppets, whose faces move and who seem to speak, have begun to appear on stage and elsewhere. These puppets open up extraordinary new possibilities that go beyond the scope of this book, but the design principles described so far, which suggest that the forms of all aspects of a puppet can be developed out of the character's core color or colors, are still entirely relevant, as they speak to the essence of the human being, whatever form the puppet may take.

'Alifanfaron,' a giant & simpleton

« 'Spixy,' a wicked witch

'Rombo,' a cobbler

VII
SCENERY

"Suppose within the girdle of these walls

Are now confin'd two mighty monarchies..."

Henry V, Prologue

When I was working on *The Moon and Sixpence*, an opera about the artist Gauguin based on the novel of the same name by Somerset Maugham, the stage designer created one of the sets in imitation of the painter's style. Gauguin's paintings are vibrant, they are full of green foliage and exotic flowers and their colors are strong. Once these images had been transferred onto flats, they immediately took hold of the stage space and filled it with the tropical rainforest; other scenes that depicted Parisian streets and houses had been painted in muted monotones and had nothing like the same power. The contrast of the urban and country settings gave a strong sense of Gauguin's need to break free of the restrictions of the city and find freedom in the jungle, so that he could begin to paint in ways that allowed him to be true to himself and his art. The entire stage picture made such an impression on me that I can recall it half a century later. But it had one major drawback: This particular set was complete in its own right, so much so that the singers were a distraction and prevented me from enjoying the riot of colors and forms behind them.

I realized from this peculiar experience that a set must allow the actors to complete the picture and not compete with them for the audience's attention. When later working for professional theatre and opera companies, I discovered that one of the factors that determined whether an overall design succeeded or failed was whether the team of costume, set and lighting designers competed or cooperated with each other.

COLOR

When we enter a space, the first thing we usually experience, though often unconsciously, is its **mood** or **atmosphere** that has been created by the surrounding colors. Then we might begin to become aware of the **space** itself, of its dimensions and forms and their qualities. If this awareness of the space continues, we may also notice the **perspective**. The application of color in the set can be the means by which these three elements—mood, the sense of space and perspective—are created on the stage.

1. MOODS OR ATMOSPHERES

Colors can affect and influence our feelings profoundly just because our initial response to them is unconscious, and the earliest distinction we make of which we may be aware is between warm and cool tones. Warm colors are welcoming and draw us out of ourselves, be-

cause they allow us to feel secure when we are surrounded by them. When they are intensified they may have the opposite effect and become threatening. Cool colors can arouse feelings of sadness and loneliness or isolation, because they throw us back upon ourselves. They can also be experienced as threatening when the colors increase in intensity. When warm and cool colors balance each other in a space, we as spectators have a greater freedom to experience both the space and ourselves in it.

2. SPACE

In relation to space, color can have two main effects: It can make the space bigger or smaller, and it can evoke a sense of well-being or a lack of it in the individual looking at it. Warm tones push into and fill the stage space and can crowd out anything else present. Cool tones widen the stage space and can give the impression of emptiness. It can be helpful to work with this fundamental contrast when creating two distinct areas of the stage to accommodate different actions that are happening at the same time.

3. PERSPECTIVE

Color can have a powerful influence on how an audience experiences the perspective of the set: When the scene needs greater depth than the actual size the stage provides, stronger blues and lavenders at the front that recede into softer and paler shades at the back of the stage give the illusion of infinite distances. If the designer places a building or a half-indoor set in intense reds and browns in the foreground, the illusion of distance will be stronger. Changing the perspective in the course of the play, by bringing cool tones forward and placing the warmer shades at the back may cause confusion or discomfort in the audience and go so far as to alter or disrupt their breathing.

4. TONES

When working with either contrasting or similar colors, it is important to define each area of color as clearly as possible. This is because this definition helps to prevent the whole set image from acquiring a general dullness and the colors appearing blurred from the back of the auditorium. Contrasting or complementary colors can create liveliness in the set images. They can also make the impression that the space is confused and chaotic. Strongly clashing colors can look brash. Colors similar in tone, such as those in the rainbow sequence, enhance each other; this in turn creates harmony and possibly a certain naïveté. If only similar colors are used, they can become bland and will appear boring. When the tone is varied within a given color, intense areas glow and reach forward, while pale areas recede.

TEXTURE

In general, texture speaks to the sense of touch and in any observer can awaken the emotions of sympathy and antipathy with directness, though the audience will not necessarily be aware of them. When textures are used effectively in a set, the viewer may have such an experience without having to actually touch the surfaces. When applying textures to a set, the main tool is the contrast between rough and smooth surfaces.

Rough surfaces: An uneven texture absorbs the light and creates tiny shadows between the raised areas, so that the overall effect is darker than the original color. A texture that is both rough and hard creates an impression of abrasiveness, such as that of brick or rusty metal. Rough and soft textures in the same object, such as in a rustic woollen curtain, convey warmth.

Smooth surfaces: A smooth texture reflects the light and makes the setting appear paler than the original colors. An extremely smooth texture may look polished and reflect the light. Regardless of whether it is applied to a hard wall or floor or to soft drapes and curtains, a smooth surface appears cool.

STYLE

From the outset, the setting of any production invites the audience into a space that they do not yet know, into a world in which anything can happen. At the same time the setting can give clues as to what is about to happen. As a general rule, the style of the set makes an essential contribution to both the structure and framework of the production in the same way as the skeleton gives structure to the human body. The following points that the designer may want to consider can be best applied to designing for a stage with a proscenium arch, behind which the majority of the action takes place. Designing for the increasingly popular thrust stage, for theatre in the round and for open-air productions probably requires other approaches, though the principles described below will still apply and can be easily modified.

1. CONTRAST

The historically realistic or imaginary period in which the production is to be set obviously determines the overall style. Maintaining the same style of setting throughout a production ensures that the audience's focus is on the story and on the interaction between the characters. A brief contrast in style that breaks the convention already established can highlight an individual situation and allow the audience to breathe out for a moment. For example, when Hamlet visits his mother in her private chamber for a conversation, an intimate and frivolous Rococo set in a riot of warm colors can offset the cold, dark and austere spaces in the mediaeval castle at Elsinore that are the play's basic setting. A set consisting of abstract shapes that create a neutral effect provides the designer with the opportunity to include contrasting mobile objects specific to each scene; using these can simplify the general flow of the play.

2. DIRECTIONS

There are three basic spatial directions that inform and influence the style of the set, and a designer may use each of them in both straight and rounded forms. **Up/down** or the **vertical** line or plane echoes the uprightness of the human being and has the potential to inwardly lift the audience. It also suggests man-made structures, such as buildings and cityscapes. **Right/left** or the **horizontal** line or plane suggests open spaces; it widens the stage and allows the audience to expand also. In everyday life, looking at the ocean conveys a similar experience. **Front/back**, sometimes called the **sagittal plane** of space, offers a dynamic interchange between the outer and inner worlds and may be used to convey supernatural events. The **diagonal**, the meeting of the vertical and horizontal, can perhaps be seen as an image of the interaction between the characters. It can also create a mood that resembles the verdant world of nature. In a woodland scene, tall pine trees allow the space to seem cool and open, while beech trees, with low spreading branches, make it sheltered and perhaps secretive.

3. UP- OR DOWNSIZING DIMENSIONS

There are a number of ways to increase or diminish a performing space. If the playing space is to appear smaller, a large part of the stage can be left empty and a small set placed in one area. The whole stage can be filled with only a portion of the set, creating the impression that the playing space is too large for the actual stage. When creating landscapes or seascapes, a greatly exaggerated perspective can increase the illusion of distance. It can create the same illusion for indoor spaces, for example, to create a long ballroom or hallway that is larger than the stage allows.

SPECIFIC STAGE AREAS

1. FLOOR

A solid base under the actors' feet unconsciously gives them—and therefore the audience—security, so that the latter can freely enter the world of the play. Plain floors allow the actors to be clearly visible. A patterned floor, such as that of a checkerboard, competes for the audience's attention, and an actor wearing a black costume, for example, distracts the audience from entering the overall story when he or she moves from a black to a white square.

2. ROSTRA / STEPS / STAIRS

The use of rostra or ramps raises the floor level in strategic areas of the stage and so changes the rhythm and dynamic of the actors' movements. The variety of physical actions created

in this way can stimulate and awaken the audience's interest and also raise the importance of those moments when actors perform on rostra. The use of steps or longer staircases adds more floor levels and strengthens or emphasizes the changes in the dynamic of the movements further still. Rostra lend height to a building and can be used for either its inside or outside. They also create the opportunity for the kind of sweeping entrances down a staircase known so well from film.

3. WALLS

Walls in a set may be built for the scene or overall production or they may be simply indicated by the sides of the stage and set pieces, such as flats. Unbroken walls in an indoor setting create an atmosphere of security but can also make the space claustrophobic, so can be useful for creating the inside of a prison. When applied to outdoor scenes, solid walls appear forbidding, as the external walls of any mediaeval castle demonstrate. When decorating the walls, height or breadth can be emphasized with a stripe effect.

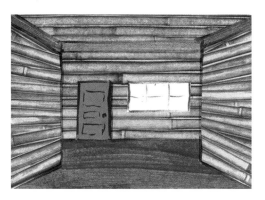

4. WINDOWS

Windows offer opportunities for further defining the style. They may open up a vista that expands the spectator's awareness of the space, especially if the weather and time of day are defined by lighting from outside the set. However, windows can draw the gaze backwards and forwards between the two so that the audience's attention is taken away from the central action, expecting events to occur outside. One window placed in the surrounding walls creates a strong point of focus. Many windows give the setting an atmosphere of airiness. Tall windows may suggest elegance on the one hand and narrowness on the other. Broad windows can create an impression of comfort and simplicity; they can also make a setting look impoverished.

5. DOORS

Doors provide another opportunity to illustrate a specific style or period. They also emphasize the comings and goings of the actors so that the audience can more readily imagine the space beyond what is visible on stage. Many doors on

a stage may create a sense of comedy or farce, especially when the audience hears them opening and closing. Exits and entrances without doors between different pieces of the set make the comings and goings less obvious and can help to create an atmosphere of deception or stealth.

6. CEILING / ROOF

Overhead scenery obscures the lighting, and so caution is advised when using it because the open space above the heads of the actors leaves the imagination of the audience free to complete the stage picture. If a scene cloth or roof structure is essential for the overall image, a heavy and low roof or ceiling seems to press down on the actors. If a light and high structure is designed, it may appear to lift the actors off their feet.

ELEMENTS OF SET

1. THE CYCLORAMA

Cyc is the conventional abbreviation for the word cyclorama, a solid, curved wall of unpainted stretched fabric, wood or plaster, usually colored white or black, at the back of the playing area of the stage and which remains a fixture throughout the production. Most white cycs help to create moods of dawn or dusk and other weather conditions when combined with colored lighting. The open space created by the cyc awakens the impression of endless distances, either when covered in part by scenery or when fully visible. A black cyclorama swallows all colored lighting, and dark costumes disappear into the dark background. The consequence can be that the heads and hands of the actors appear to float. Fabrics with strong textures, such as silk, velvet or brocade, are the only ones to remain visible even if the fabric color is dark.

2. BACKDROPS

This is the name given to the large, flat sheets of strong canvas that are usually painted and then weighted by slotting long metal pipes into their length both at the top and the bottom edges. They can be hung at any depth of the stage and cover its entire width and height, serving as a background for any scene and providing an alternative to a cyc. If the stage has a fly tower that serves as a storage space for backdrops, the design can include the use of several that

can easily be lowered or raised. The further forward the backdrop is hung, the more intimate the space becomes.

3. FLY SHEETS

These are short, wide pieces of canvas that are hung from long, strong bars or poles, such as scaffolding pipes, across and above the stage. Their primary purpose is to hide the overhead lighting units, but they can also play a part in creating an artistic mood on the stage. When the bottom edge of the fly sheet is straight, the hard line can make the scene look sharp and rectangular, and the space above the actor's head becomes heavy. If the lower edge curves slightly upwards towards the center, the line still appears straight, but the same space above becomes lighter. An irregular, 'leafy' edge softens the line of the fly sheets and can be effective in woodland scenes.

4. FLATS

A flat is the term given to a wooden frame made in a variety of sizes that, when covered with heavy, tightly stretched calico or canvas, creates a flat canvas. It is usually painted, first with white emulsion, so that this neutral base can become the foundation onto which colors and textures are added. The flat surfaces lend themselves to an abstract style of set, in front of which actors do not appear to be an intrusion. Painting three-dimensional imagery, such as a tree or the façade of a building, onto two-dimensional surfaces suggests a simple or naïve realism which at the same time allows the audience to engage imaginatively. If the set is to be

« *Ophelia with Hamlet*

in a realistic style, the same tree or building needs to be constructed in three dimensions.

5. CURTAINS OR TABS

Curtains or tabs are large pieces of soft fabric that can be used as an alternative to flats; they are sometimes gathered at the top, so as to create folds. A curtain is a simple tool to separate one area of the stage from another. The soft, three-dimensional surface created by the folds of a curtain brings warmth and intimacy to a space. If curtains fill a space entirely, they can create a claustrophobic atmosphere. For example, in the three indoor scenes in *As You Like It*, an excessive use of curtains can convey the fact that Duke Frederick's tyrannical and unpredictable brother has made the court a place where no one can speak freely.

6. GAUZES OR SCRIMS

Gauzes are large, loosely woven, semi-transparent curtains that are stretched taut on rods or frames and suspended using pulleys that can be

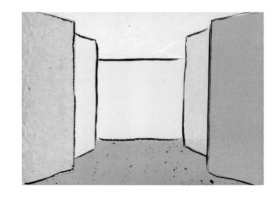

painted in a similar way to backdrops. They are used to divide the stage into different areas that can be seen separately or at the same time. When lit by strip lights positioned in the downstage wings, the gauze becomes opaque, and only the stage space in front is visible. When lit with strip lights and spotlights positioned center front as well, the gauze becomes semi-transparent. When no light is shone on its front and the space behind is illuminated, the gauze becomes completely transparent, so that both spaces are visible, but the back becomes the focus. When both spaces can be seen at the same time, the gauze allows each to have its own quality or mood; it can be particularly useful in scenes in which the metaphysical world is present at the same time as the physical.

7. DRAPES

These are pieces of soft fabric gathered at the top into folds that serve as set accessories at windows and doors. They can be used to soften indoor settings. Light, silky drapes that catch the light when hanging at windows lend a feminine, elegant touch to the set. Heavy velvet fabric that absorbs the light creates a formal, masculine space. Long, full curtains suggest opulence and wealth. Short, skimpy drapes give the sense of hard times and constricting circumstances. In the same way as stage curtains, drapes may be used to divide a space, but within interior settings only, when contrasting events take place simultaneously. The 'arras,' or drape, for example, in *Hamlet* separates one small part of the stage from the main area so that Polonius can eavesdrop on Hamlet's conversation with his mother.

8. FLOOR CLOTHS

Floor cloths are large pieces of canvas, which are usually painted and stretched across the floor and can be used to give focus to the action and to establish a clear performing space when it is not identical with the size of the actual stage. Using a floor cloth has two positive aspects: It reduces the sound of actors' footsteps and eliminates the dangers that accompany slippery floor surfaces. The size, color, texture, shape and position of the floor cloth, both individually and in combination with other elements of the set, create a broad spectrum of atmospheres.

9. FURNITURE

Furniture designed and built specifically for a production and in keeping with its style is always more effective than ready-made or second-hand pieces. A stage devoid of furniture emphasizes the emptiness of the space and creates a mood of either openness or isolation. Chairs, tables and other items of furniture can

appear to clutter the space and limit the actors' movements, creating an atmosphere of confinement or perhaps oppression. When the furniture required is in harmony with the style of the entire set, the space appears balanced. When the furniture is in contrast to other aspects of the set, tension is created. The placement of the furniture should lead the audience's eye to the center of the action. Designing pieces of furniture that can be used in more than one way—a bed that serves as a tower, a bench and a wall, for example—brings both simplicity and effectiveness to any set.

10. DÉCOR

Scenery, curtains and furniture can be highlighted with an unlimited variety of patterned designs, adding style and focus. But beware of too much, especially in clashing styles, unless deliberately choosing that look.

11. PROPERTIES OR PROPS

Properties are smaller objects required on stage as part of the play's action, such as walking sticks, tea sets, fans, bags and letters, and are also known as props. As with the larger items of furniture, props made specifically for the production are, in general, more effective than those ready-made, as the opportunity to work with color, texture and style are simply greater. Generally props should be in proportion with the rest of the scene, but exaggerated sizes can add humor. Props made smaller, on the other hand, can become difficult for the audience to see. Ideally, props should be made available to the actors as soon as possible for rehearsals.

VIII
LIGHTING

"How far that little candle throws his beams!

So shines a good deed in a naughty world."

The Merchant of Venice, Act V, scene 1

The school where my parents were teachers was evacuated during the war, and so my family moved to a large country house with unused farm buildings on the grounds in a small town on the west coast of England. My parents transformed a grain loft above the stable block into our new home. Once this was done, my father, a true handyman, set about transforming the stables below us into a simple theatre for school assemblies and plays by removing the partitions between the looseboxes and installing an electric power supply. He was inspired by his friend Michael Wilson, who for many years had worked on how to use color in lighting, and one day he began to build what are known as saltwater dimmers for a simple stage lighting system.

Somehow he acquired—not an easy task during the war—nine accumulator jars (not unlike large, tall, rectangular vases) and fitted a copper plate (the permanent contact or electrode) into the base of each of them. He then joined a length of copper wire to the plate, led the wire to the top of the jar, which he would later connect to the electric power supply. His next step was to fit copper cups to the bottom of Aladdin lamp glasses (four for each jar) and to place these inside each accumulator jar so that they all stood on the copper plate. He then hung a three-inch long, barrel-shaped copper tube (the moveable contact or electrode) from a pulley above the jar. The pulley allowed the tubes to be lowered into and lifted out of each of the Aladdin glasses. Finally, he attached conductor wires to the metal tubes, connected these to the power supply, filled the jar with water and a measure of salt to make the brine, and the dimmers were ready for use. To vary the lighting levels, the barrel-shaped metal tube was lowered towards the copper cup and plate, and the closer it came to them, the stronger the light grew. Unfortunately, the deeper the tube was lowered, the hotter the solution became, and the gurgling of the water grew so loud that the tube had to be raised as quickly as possible to lower the temperature again and reduce the sound level (and, sadly, the lighting level, too).

I cannot remember how the individual lamps were connected to the dimmers, but I can still see my father cutting plywood levers for the pulleys and painting on them the colors of the colored gels to be installed. Once the dimmers were working, my father built floodlights by cutting holes in extremely large metal biscuit tins and made the frames for individual color gels out of the tin lids, wire and a lot of ingenuity.

We do not, in general, see light itself, but we do see both the objects that light touches and the shadows the light creates when it meets the object, whether this is an actor, a backdrop or a piece of furniture. This means that lighting a stage is as much about the play of shadows that are created as it is about making objects visible in clear light.

Lighting for a theatre production therefore has two main aims: at a basic level, to make the actors and the action visible to the audience, but also, of equal importance, to create atmospheres and moods. These potentially contrasting goals need to be in the designer's mind throughout the design process. Too much light on the stage makes a scene everyday or bland and washes out the shadows; too little, accompanied by strong shadows, and the audience's eyes will strain to see the action. As with all other aspects of the production, designing and then creating the sequence of lighting changes is about applying the artistic principle—that the inner life of the play can be given physical expression, in atmospheres, for example—to the practical demands of the production.

The stronger the contrasts are in color and texture, style and form in the lighting, the more dramatic the production becomes. At the same time, the drama created by the contrasts between the lightest and darkest areas can be softened and harmonious moods created with just small changes in the color, texture and form of the lighting. So designing the lighting for a production consists of working with the principles of contrast and balance or harmony at every phase of the performance. Once this aspect of the design has been addressed, the changes from one image, scene and act to the next need to be as fluid and smooth as possible so that they can be unobtrusive in those places where that is the designer's choice.

Finally, in contrast to the time-consuming efforts needed to first create and then make alterations to finished set, props and costumes, it is quite normal and a standard procedure that the lighting design is only realized in the last few rehearsal days. One of the reasons for this is that lighting settings can be adjusted quickly when changes need to be made, and many an unsatisfying moment in the initial design can be positively transformed with only small and simple shifts in the color, texture, type, source and level of lighting. It is also only in the end phase of a production that the designer can consciously see the relationships between the light-

ing and the other components of the production, such as set, props and costumes, and continue to make adjustments that enable these relationships to become a true expression of the life of the play.

COLOR

A lot of lighting that simply makes objects visible is created by the light from neutral instruments and appears much like daylight. Colors build atmospheres and intensify moods created by the performers, giving any setting a psychological dimension. As a designer it is helpful to approach colors in lighting as if they were pigments or paints with which the surfaces on the stage are 'painted.' However, the colors in

three-dimensional lighting are governed by principles different from those of the two-dimensional canvas.

1. PRIMARY & COMPLEMENTARY COLORS

Six colors make up the entire lighting color spectrum: **three primary colors** and their more metaphysical counterparts, **three complementary colors**. In contrast to those used in set and costumes, red, blue and yellow, the three primary colors in lighting are **red**, **blue** and **green**. The primary colors are stark. Using them to light the stage creates strong atmospheres and dramatic effects and brings a dynamic quality to the lighting of specific scenes or areas of the stage that an audience may notice. The **complementary** color for **red** is **turquoise** or **cyan**, for

blue, **lemon yellow** and for **green**, **magenta**; these are the colors that are only seen in the shadows created when colors in the lighting instruments shine on objects that block one or other of the colors. As the illustrations show, when one of the primary colors is reduced or completely removed, the remaining two make the complementary colors seen in the shadows more intense. When only one primary color

lights the stage, the shadows appear black. If all three primary colors are fitted as colored filters into the same lamp, no light shines through and the stage remains **black**. If the same primary colors are fitted into separate instruments and they light the same area of a white surface, the three colors cancel each other out and the stage becomes **white**.

The primary colors also change the colors painted onto scenery and of costume fabrics. A **red** light on a green surface creates a black surface, on a red surface creates a white surfacea and on a blue surface warms the blue. In the same way a **green** light on a red surface creates a black surface, on a green surface creates a white surface and on a blue surface cools the blue. The primary color of **blue** does not create such extreme contrasts: A blue light on a green surface softens the green, on a red surface softens the red and on a blue surface dilutes the blue. A **yellow** light (not a primary color) dulls the entire stage.

2. COLOR FILTERS

When complementary colors are required to create atmospheres, not just as shadows, color filters can be used. When filters create the colored light, the shadows that appear on colored surfaces are subtle and extremely varied in tone, and an audience will probably not be aware of them.

TEXTURE

The texture of a beam of light from any lamp can be altered in two main ways: 1) by making or buying templates of specific shapes, known as **gobos**, to mask part of the light beam. They can be inserted, for example, into ERS or profile spotlights (see Lighting Instruments) to create windows instead of having a solid window built. Other standardized gobos create images such as trees, buildings and cityscapes. 2) by using gobos in lamps with a rotating facility (see Moving Head Lights) that then create moving images, such as clouds. Special lighting effects created by gobos give focus to an important moment in a play, but they are most effective when used sparingly if they are not to distract the audience's attention away from the action and make the scene restless.

Another way of creating textures is to combine the lighting with a sculptured or textured surface or object, such as a piece of scenery. If the surface is lit with color washes coming from more than one angle using strip lights and a variety of filters are used, the same sculptured or textured surface or object can change its appearance in many ways. If profile spotlights are added to create specific focus, the possibilities become limitless.

STYLE

As a general principle, the less obtrusive the lighting is for the majority of a production, the more effective any strong lighting effects will be to highlight dramatic moments and create contrasts. Three elements of style create variety in lighting: the **type** of lighting instrument, the **source** of light, the **level** of lighting. Strip lights, for example, illuminate the whole stage, while spotlights light specific areas. Lighting from below or the sides creates indoor settings, and a lighting wash mainly from above sets the scene for an outdoor environment such as a street or forest.

LIGHTING INSTRUMENTS

There are two basic types of lighting instruments: manually controlled lanterns, generally termed 'generics or **generic** lights,' and those remotely controlled, called '**intelligent** lights.' Generics are generally divided into two groups: those that create broad washes of light, **strip lights**, and those that light specific areas, **spotlights**.

1. GENERIC LIGHTS

Strip lights: Strip lights or basic floodlights are the simplest form of lighting for a stage and are used to create wide and open washes of light. They are made of square boxes that when joined together become one oblong housing; each box has one of its sides open. Strip lights have no lenses that focus or intensify the beam of light but can have a frame attached to the open side into which a color filter can be slotted. As a batten, strip lights can be hung from a bar above the stage and flood the stage floor with light. A line of strip lights hung and tilted is useful for general lighting for the cyclorama or backdrop; such strip lights are called 'cyc' lights. Strip lights can also be placed on the floor along the front edge of the stage for use as footlights.

PAR-cans: PAR-cans are instruments with a sealed beam and a high level of brightness. In the past they were the main instruments used for lighting rock and pop events, for which strong primary colors and flat white light were what was required. In the theatre they are used to create powerful beams of side, top or back lighting and for washes of strong color and other special effects. PAR-cans come in a number of widths: very narrow, narrow, medium and wide. Because of their low cost, light weight, easy maintenance and high durability, they are often used in combination with stage smoke to make visible the path of the light beam.

Mini PAR-cans or Birdies: As a form of mini PAR-can, using only 12 volts, the small size of 'birdies' means that they can be hidden behind furniture and scenery and positioned close to the area to be lit, to create a spotlight or color wash for a small area of the stage. Another of their advantages is that they can be mounted on the front of the stage without blocking the audience's view.

2. SPOTLIGHTS

ERSs: Ellipsoidal Reflector Spotlights, also known as profile spotlights, give, as their name implies, a clear edge to the light beam and are therefore used to light specific areas of the stage. The beam edge can be cut off with even greater precision if they are used in combination with flexible shutters or barn doors (see below). For example, the beam of a spotlight can be cut to fit exactly inside the frame of the door to pick out a character in a doorway. If the beam has been given a clear edge with a barn door shutter, the spotlight lens can be adjusted further, either to retain the sharpness or to throw the light out of focus.

Fresnels: The main feature of a Fresnel is that it has a specific Fresnel lens that gives a soft edge to the beam of light; this beam can also be narrowed or widened by adjusting the lens. Fresnel lenses can operate close to the light source, so the actual lanterns tend to be small. They are often used in groups, but it is useful if the Fresnels can be individually controlled, so that the soft light can be more clearly directed into the main acting areas of the performing space. A Fresnel instrument can be used, for example, to create a soft pool or shaft of light on a particular actor. If a more controlled beam of light is required and no ERS spotlights are available, a barn door (see below) can be attached to the front of the Fresnel.

LEDs: An LED or 'light-emitting diode' is a crystal the size of a grain of sugar that gives off light from its top surface. While once LEDs could not produce strong light, in recent years the brightness of multi-color LED lights has increased and they can now be used for lighting all types of performances. The units used for the stage have been mainly three-color RGB (red, green and blue) units; their limitation was that they could not produce a good yellow. But now most manufacturers are producing good quality RGBAW (red, green, blue, amber and white) LEDs. LEDs have a number of advantages: They use only approximately 40–60 watts per unit compared to 1000 watts for a standard PAR-can, they do not require conventional dimmers because they are dimmed digitally and the professional range of LEDs today allows almost any color to be mixed.

3. INTELLIGENT LIGHTS

Moving Head Lights: Moving head lights are remotely controlled instruments that during a performance can be moved and then focused on to any part of the stage. Conventionally they have pan and tilt motors and a number of fixed color filters inside or a color mixing system of moving color wheels. They are manufactured either as ERS spotlights or Fresnels, and may have fitted gobos that spin, have prism effects and be put in or out of focus. As they can be focused almost anywhere and refocused from the lighting control board as often as is needed during a performance, they can easily reduce the number of lighting instruments a production needs. Moving head lights are the most versatile and powerful pieces of lighting equipment available today. When used in combination with stage smoke, they sculpt the light and add the third dimension. However, they are expensive and the motors are noisy, which can be distracting. They are also considerably heavier than generic lanterns and take time to program, but once set up they can be left to take care of themselves.

Finally, an all-round lighting rig for a stage may consist of strip lights, ERS spotlights, Fresnels and LEDs that can create strong color moods. A selection of other instruments that light specific areas of the stage can be added to this basic set-up.

4. LIGHTING ACCESSORIES

Filters or Gels: To color the beam of light, transparent colored sheets, cut to the size required, are slotted into the frame attached to the front of each lamp. 'Gel' refers to the gelatine from which they were originally manufactured but which crumpled and melted if the lamp became too hot and were therefore a fire hazard. Today they are made of flexible plastic and called 'filters.'

Barn Doors: Barn doors are metal frames with four individually adjustable shutters that can be slotted onto the front of all instruments. They are a useful addition to any lighting instrument to mask unwanted light spillage. They have four individual hinges so that each shutter can be adjusted to the specific angle required.

Above / Overhead

THE SOURCE OF LIGHT

Any light draws the audience's attention to the area to which it is directed, and if the lighting of that area is to be balanced, it must be lit from different sides of the stage. When the lighting level is stronger from one direction than from others, any moods created by the actors, set and costumes can be heightened. Thus, where the instruments lighting the stage are placed has an influence on their effects. The main positions are above and below, the front and the back, and the left and the right of the stage.

1. THE FRONT

Lighting directly from the front clearly illumines a specific area, such as an actor's face, but it also makes the area appear flat and blinds the performers. If the light is directed slightly from the left or the right, the face retains more form and character. If the entire stage is lit mainly from the front, the moving shadows behind the actor draw the audience's attention away from the acting. If front light is important for a scene, instruments with softer edges to the light

Below

beams, such as Fresnels, will soften the shadows and blend them with the background.

2. ABOVE/OVERHEAD

Light from above creates a daytime mood; the atmosphere becomes social when the light fills the entire stage. When only one instrument shines from above, the space appears empty and isolates actors or actions taking place in it. The shadows that one light creates on the floor may be minimal, but faces appear hollow and ghostlike when one spotlight from above is the only source of light. This use of a single spotlight from above heightened a particularly dramatic moment in a production of *King Lear*: After Cornwall and his wife had maliciously blinded Gloucester, a dark stage and one spotlight with a red filter that shone on him alone emphasized the fact that his empty eye sockets had become *'dark and comfortless.'*

3. BELOW

Light from below has an intimate, inward quality and, when used to fill the stage, creates the atmosphere of an evening at home or a campfire outdoors where the dark invites those present to confide their inmost thoughts and feelings. Light from below on a specific area of the stage also creates an atmosphere of conspiracy or threat and is useful, for example, to heighten moments when a plot is being hatched. On an otherwise darkened stage, one or two instruments lighting the space from below creates a ghostly atmosphere. A row of footlights along the front of the stage may seem to be a barrier between the audience and actors, but when used skillfully it can build a bridge that allows greater interaction between the two.

4. LEFT & RIGHT

Floodlights positioned either on the right or the left create an atmosphere of dawn or dusk and cast long shadows across the stage floor. A single shaft of light from a spotlight at either side of the stage creates an inner space. In the same way, light from house left/stage right illuminating the house right/stage left side of the stage emphasises the outer aspects of a situation; light from house right/stage left illuminating house left/stage right creates intimacy and inwardness. For example, when Sir Toby Belch and his friends in *Twelfth Night* sit house right/ stage left and are lit from house left/stage right, the setting and the lighting create the atmosphere of an indoor drinking parlor; when Viola stands house left/stage right, mourning the loss of her twin brother or dreaming of her love, Duke Orsino, light on her from house right/ stage left heightens the intensity of her feelings.

5. THE BACK/BEHIND

Light from the back of the stage creates silhouettes of and halos around actors and scenery; stage smoke can enhance this effect. If the front of the stage is dark and the back is lit, the illumined area at the back deepens and expands the entire stage space, creating the impression of a tunnel. However, when lights shine from the back of the stage into the auditorium, it is important not to blind the audience. One way to counter the problems that back lighting often causes is to use one strong main color from the back and a soft fill light from the front in an opposite color.

If a piece of the set is lit from behind, the contrasts create the third dimension. This style of

House left / Stage right

House right / Stage left

Back lighting

lighting is useful when a gauze is used to separate one part of the stage from another when staging a dream or vision. Back lighting was used in the same production of *King Lear* already mentioned: When the blinded Gloucester stood at the imagined cliff edge, ready to throw himself off, light from the back created a halo around his head that darkened his sightless eyes and gave the audience the sense that they were standing beside him.

LIGHTING LEVELS

As the third of the elements that create style or form in lighting, the level of light is as important as the choice of lighting instrument and the source of light. In addition, the colors of the filters play a significant role when setting the lighting levels; the darker the color, the higher the lighting level needs to be. A deep tone or dark color in the lighting may indeed create the mood or atmosphere of a scene, but the lighting level may need to be raised and the color intensity reduced so that the audience and actors feel that they can see what is happening.

The shadows also play their part in determining the level of the lighting. The light needs to be strong enough that the shadows—both the dark areas of the stage and the colored shadows created by the mixtures of colors used—do not dominate the light areas. If, before the design is implemented, a number of lights have been well distributed throughout the playing space and the highlights and shadows balanced so that there are no dark holes or glaring patches, then the stage has an effective basic level of lighting which can then be adapted to whatever the design requires.

An effectively lit stage not only helps actors feel comfortable on stage, it also allows an audience to enjoy the performance. Installing some soft low lighting in the auditorium for the performance also helps actors maintain their relationship to the audience, especially when the level of lighting on stage is low.

TO SUM UP:

Lighting a play, when all the instruments have been hung and filters installed, is like painting on a moving, three-dimensional canvas when both the visible actions and the inner life of a production are continuously changing. After many years of working with the principles, I can only describe my personal experience of attempting to illuminate the actors in their costumes—with their colors, textures and styles when they are moving within the colors, textures and styles of the set in ways that enhance their artistic work—as having the privilege and responsibility of placing the cherry on top of the cake.

IX

APPLICATION & EXAMPLES

"How many goodly creatures are there here!

How beauteous mankind is! O brave new world,

That has such people in't..."

The Tempest, Act V, scene 1

When I was working for the Royal Shakespeare Company, one of my responsibilities was to return the costumes made for past productions to their proper places in the storage space after they had been dry-cleaned. I often wondered what the future held for them. Were these creations of years gone by all waiting to appear on stage again? I later saw a play performed by a new, young company, and, as usual, before the production began I searched the program for the names of those who had designed the show and made the costumes. I found no mention of either designer or backstage staff, but when the performance began, the questions I had asked in the RSC wardrobe were answered, as I recognized a costume on stage as one I had made all those years ago.

Chapters 2 to 4 describe the three principles at the heart of the design process, and chapters 5 to 8 set out how to use them in the individual fields of costume, makeup, set and lighting. But anyone wishing to incorporate these principles into an actual design may find it difficult to envisage what happens when the three elements of color, texture and style are applied to all of the four fields, let alone to imagine how each interacts with the other three. So the following examples of application taken from productions I have designed may help to move the inner pictures from the world of the imagination into colors, materials and forms and to transform the two-dimensional sketches into three-dimensional objects—curtains, furniture, costumes and props—living in a stage space.

INTRODUCTION/ BACKGROUND

The following points give the specific background to the descriptions of each play and the design choices made.

The Plays: The descriptions of the plays, their settings and characters express my individual artistic approach to each production. There is no attempt to be all-inclusive. I have selected just one or more characters from each play and described the principles as applied to one or more costumes worn by these characters at particular moments.

Colors: The plays are not in chronological sequence; their order is determined by the quality and nature of the colors used in each production, starting with dark, indistinct tones and moving on to those of greater intensity and stronger contrasts.

The Stage: The designs were made for a space that had no side curtains, backdrop or tabs. The basic elements used to create the stage were: 1m x 2m flats, a cyclorama and a paintable, non-slip floor.

Costumes: Following the descriptions of the design are the descriptions of some of the experiences of individual actors when wearing the costumes.

MACBETH

THE PLAY

We find ourselves in a murky fog on a lonely heath when the play opens. The swirling
"… filthy air"
is robbed of color and only grey shapes seem to move about within it; these are the three witches, who have gathered to observe and find ways of confusing those they encounter. No distinctions exist between them; their words of prophetic doom sound as if from one voice. Macbeth stands out against this monotone lack of form. Lady Macbeth's schemes, followed by her encouragement of her husband's propensity for evil, lead them both to their inexorable and tragic ends. I was struck by the murky situation and the power of superstition at the opening of the play and wondered about Macbeth's state of mind. Why would he believe the witches' words? Further on in the play, I felt Macbeth to be ambitious, weak and lacking any sense of judgement; this allows Lady Macbeth to persuade him to murder Duncan and then follow this first murder with others.

THE DESIGN
Monotone Colors, Varied Textures, Uncoordinated Styles

For the opening of the play I created a **setting** bare of scenery apart from low-lying rocks painted in varying shades of grey. The **lighting** was cool and dim, and floor lights were used at the sides to create low-level lighting of the main playing space to create the atmosphere of a conspiracy. I envisaged the three witches as a trio dressed in **costumes** of washed-out grey rags. I cut fabrics in varying grey tones and textures into rough, shapeless pieces, draped them around the figures and then sewed them together. My aim was to blend these costumes into their setting to create an eerie effect. For Macbeth's costume I used a mixture of varied tones that created the overall effect of grey. I wanted him to appear clumsy and susceptible to his wife's evil intentions, so I made a bulky jacket from heavy tweed. In contrast, Lady Macbeth's figure-hugging dress was created out

The Witches

Lady Macbeth and Macbeth

As Queen and King

of a flowing silver satin with a brittle, semi-transparent drape in the same color. When she became queen, I added another drape in poisonous green, made of heavy, dull silk and flimsy nylon. When Lady Macbeth spoke of blood staining her hands in the sleepwalking scene, a green spotlight was shone on her from above and a red one from below. The complementary colored shadows of each light could then be seen in the jagged creases of her glass-like costume, creating an almost supernatural effect.

Macbeth: "I really enjoyed wearing this costume, because the character felt very human and real. I had a strong sense of bluster and insecure pride with the stiff, puffy chest and there was something about the tightness of the cuffs that brought my attention to my wrists. It made me feel vulnerable, and I became aware of the fact that I was being controlled and manipulated by someone else." – Matt

Lady Macbeth: "The costume almost suffocated me at the neck, and a rigid feeling in the back made me want to hold my posture very erect and immediately gave me a sense of my own regal qualities. The long, silk skirt gave my movement a fluidity and confidence. The silk was also cool against my skin and seemed to intensify the cold in the room. The green collar gave me a sense that my head was separate from my body." – Lara

A MIDSUMMER NIGHT'S DREAM

THE PLAY

Most of the play is set at night at midsummer, and both characters and audience experience the events of the play as if they are a dream. The figure of Puck, a more benign and playful manifestation of the supernatural than the witches in *Macbeth*, spreads confusion among the mortals by transforming his appearance and changing the sound of his voice. Some victims of Puck's mischief are the group of craftsmen, also referred to as 'the mechanicals.' Bottom, the weaver, is the central figure, on whose shoulders Puck places an ass's head.

The fact that there are three groups of characters caught my attention: the nobles, the mechanicals and the fairies. Each group is distinct, and I wanted to express their differences with the three color circles. For the nobles I chose pastel colors to create a degree of refine-

The Mechanicals

ment not present in the other two groups. The mechanicals, the 'salt of the earth,' I chose to dress in earth tones. I saw the fairies as embodying the entire rainbow circle of colors, bridging the worlds of the nobles and the craftsmen.

THE DESIGN
Complementary Colors, Soft Textures, Flowing Styles

For **scenery** I placed flats painted in dark blues, greens and a hint of purple around the edge of the stage. Bushes, created out of chicken wire and cloth, were added to the open space, behind which the playful Puck could vanish at will. By **lighting** the setting in soft, dim blues and greens, I wanted to create a mood of mystery. I added the impression of moonlight shining through the trees by using a couple of branch gobos without colored filters. As the actors walked through the delicate patterns of the beams created by the gobos shining on to them, the audience understood exactly where they were and at what time. For Puck's **costume** I painted the complementary colors of green

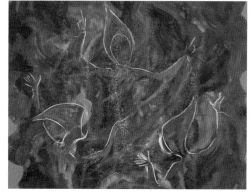

Puck

and red in chaotic, varied brush-strokes onto soft cotton fabric, and then cut this into a thigh-length, sleeveless tunic with a hood and an angular, jagged hemline to emphasize how different he was from the other fairies. These I dressed in soft, flowing gauzes in rainbow colors as a contrast. I created flowing costumes in Grecian styles for the nobles and dressed the mechanicals in a range of natural colors in autumnal tones. Their costumes were made of rough sacking and worn blankets which were cut into baggy trousers and loose smocks.

MUCH ADO ABOUT NOTHING

THE PLAY

A street bathed in sunshine in a Sicilian city is the main setting in which Dogberry, a police constable, goes about his business, accompanied by his remarkable gift for muddling his words.

Dogberry

The wide gardens and generous inner spaces of Leonato's palace under the same intense, Sicilian sun are the settings for the ongoing battle of wits that takes place between Beatrice and Benedick. I experienced the life of this play in the contrast between the more active characters, such as Beatrice and Benedick, and the more passive, such as Hero and Claudio. I chose to use bright colors for the active and pale ones for the passive. For me, Dogberry personified these contrasts.

THE DESIGN
Warm Colors, Plain Textures,
Individual Styles

The **setting** was asymmetrical and therefore off-balance: a wide street filled with elegant, pillared buildings was where Dogberry spread comic confusion. The **lighting** used was in warm, bright colors, mainly from above. To express Dogberry's muddle-headedness and bombastic style of speaking, his **costume** was a calf-length, simple tunic of rough calico, with reds and browns randomly splashed, daubed and scrubbed onto it. The tunic was stretched over a padded belly as body padding and fitted tightly. The garment's hem drooped loosely below. I added sleeves that were wide at the wrists and narrow at the shoulders both to emphasize his ample girth and to create the impression that he was on the verge of bursting out of his clothing. Beatrice was dressed in a flowing bright and warm orange floor-length dress with a tight-fitting bodice cut in Empire-style and wide at the hem. The dress had long tight sleeves with a white frill at the wrists and low round neckline. The most striking part of

Benedick's costume was a red-brown velvet jacket or tunic with a large white collar that he wore over white tights and red-brown suede boots. The cut of the jacket emphasized the upper body; the sleeves were the opposite to Dogberry's in that they were wide at the shoulders and narrow at the wrists, again to give the upper body and shoulders the focus.

Beatrice: "The dress and Empire-style bodice made this costume fun to wear. When I put it on and looked in the mirror, I was a little too pleased with how well it looked. Because of the shape of the skirt, I had to take long, arguably overconfident strides when walking, from time to time lightly kicking up the hem in front of me. The openness of the dress was balanced by the structure of the bodice and sleeves, which held my upper body firmly in place."   – Brigitte

Benedick: "The transformation into this character was virtually instantaneous once I put on the costume, and as soon as I saw myself in the mirror, my chin lifted and a smug grin appeared

Beatrice and Benedick

on my face! I loved the color and the cut and generally felt rather proud of myself." – Matt

MEASURE FOR MEASURE

THE PLAY

The story is set in the dukedom of Vienna, where the affairs of state are in disarray and the morals of its citizens lax. Lucio, a 'Fantastic,' is an outrageous, inquisitive character, similar to a wasp buzzing around other people's affairs, with a sharp wit and perceptive zeal. He often oversteps the thresholds of conventional decorum and is full of his own abilities and importance. To me this play addresses issues of right and wrong in their extreme forms. I also noted two aspects that differentiate it from other plays: the use of disguise to discover the truth and the struggle to find clarity in the darkness and confusion of the disarray. I chose to use the tension between black and white to express this theme.

THE DESIGN
Contrasting Colors, Elegant Textures, Clear-cut Styles

I built the entire design on the contrast of black and white and heightened this with other clear, bright colors. I created a geometrical **set** and added a third dimension by building abstract, rectangular bas-reliefs of different sizes and depths on the flats out of cardboard boxes, which were then painted. The **lighting** created sharp, square shadows wherever it touched the edges of the playing space and made angular patterns on the floor. Black and white placed next to each other was the basis of the **costume** designed for Lucio. I chose a geometric form for his tunic, making the lower part into a skirt of Renaissance vertical pleating that hung from a horizontal yoke. A belt emphasized the horizontal line. I stiffened the tunic by backing the geometric pleating in a heavy felt. A short, bright yellow cloak and yellow fez-shaped hat completed the costume. The cloak could fly freely from Lucio's shoulders when he sprang from one situation to the next in the play. At the front one side fell into a point, and he used this to tease other characters by picking it up and poking them with it.

Lucio

Lucio: "As soon as I put on this costume I began to prance around the stag. I kept looking at myself in the mirror and generally had a good time in it. The black and white stripes and flared skirt-like part made me feel rather jaunty and faintly ridiculous, and the hat was simply glorious in its absurdity." – Matt

HAMLET

THE PLAY

Hamlet returns home to Elsinore for his father's funeral, only to witness his mother's remarriage to his uncle almost immediately afterwards. His despair at this imprisons him until his father's ghost reveals that he has been murdered by his brother and calls on his son to avenge him. Hamlet is initially unable to act on this; yet when some visiting players prepare a short play for the new monarch, he is inspired to partly rewrite it in order to
"catch the conscience of a king."
Although he does not succeed in catching Claudius at this time, before his death Hamlet frees himself from his inner imprisonment, finding an equanimity that at last enables him to avenge his father's death.

In conversation with his childhood friends, Rosenkrantz and Gildenstern, Hamlet describes the true essence of the human being:
"What a piece of work is a man!"
He speaks of the nobility, 'infinite' faculties and other attributes that are the highest aspects of human nature. To me this is the core of the play, a nugget of truth embedded in the depths of the

deceit and treachery that surround Hamlet. I wanted to show in my design how the light of truth is able to right wrongs, even if the cost is death.

THE DESIGN
Black & White Colors, Hard & Soft Textures, Formal & Freer Styles

The contrast of outdoor and indoor scenes set up a dynamic in the **settings** of the play. For the outdoor scenes the flats were painted in tones of dark stone and straight painted lines that evoked the austerity of the castle battlements. Rostra were placed in a pentagon around the edges of the stage floor, the fifth edge being the front of the stage. An extra level of rostra lifted the floor level further at the back for the battle-

ments scenes. Flowing, deep red velvet and brocade curtains draped the flats for the indoor scenes. The indoor set was elegantly yet sparsely furnished, aimed at echoing the auster-ity of the outer scenes and capturing the mood of the entire play.

The **lighting** was in cool colors and directed from the sides and front. It became wild and stormy when lamps with gobos and blue and green filters were focused on the backdrop. Floor lights were also directed onto the back-drop to create silhouettes of the battlements; this effect heightened the general dark and tragic mood.

Hamlet is the only play in which Shakespeare indicates the color of the **costume** its protago-

nist wears; the 'inky black' helps Hamlet retain his equilibrium. However, at the moment when he becomes more alert and asks the players to include a new speech in their upcoming per-formance, I gave him a short, black cloak with a harsh white lining. When Hamlet returns from England with proof of his uncle's capacity for deceit, I dressed him entirely in white. I chose stiff textures to indicate the formality of royalty and used heavy brocade and velvet for Hamlet's first doublet, hose and cloak and softer and more light-weight fabrics for his second costume. The clear-cut Renaissance style was chosen to highlight Hamlet's awakened consciousness in both costumes, the first more literal in style than the second.

CYMBELINE

THE PLAY

Cymbeline is set at the time when Caesar Augus-tus ruled over the Roman Empire and was grad-ually colonizing large areas of Europe, demand-ing high taxes from his new subjects. Cymbeline, the ruling King of Britain, is unaware that the queen, his second wife, is drugging him; it clouds his judgment, and because he unjustifia-bly refuses to pay what he rightfully owes to Rome, the two nations find themselves in con-flict. To me, the dynamic between light and warmth expressed the tension between Britain and Rome; the fire of the Roman Empire wanted to devour the light of Britain. I also realized that Caesar Augustus was Emperor at the time of the birth of Christ-Jesus, in whom light and warmth live in harmony. The conflict at the heart of the

80

Hamlet

play then became the theme of my design. The mood and characters of the British north lived in yellows and light tones and those of the Roman south in reds and deeper shades.

THE DESIGN
Warm & Light Colors, Elaborate & Plain Textures, Rigid & Unformed Styles

The **set** depicted the rough stonework of Cymbeline's castle in soft, pale tones so that indoor and outdoor scenes could alternate in quick succession. Artificial branches, rough logs, rocks made of wire netting and sacking and a cave, built out of irregularly-shaped wooden structures, created the woodland scenes. Those in Rome were performed in a confined space on an apron stage with no set. The **lighting** was the main tool used to distinguish the worlds of Britain and Rome. Soft greens and blues created the mood for the light of Britain, and by positioning spotlights fitted with leaf gobos and pale green filters on the floor at the side of the stage, the impression was created that the woods of Britain and later of Wales were filled with sunlight. Strong oranges and reds in the confined apron space then created the atmosphere of the heat and dust of the city of Rome.

Two thousand years ago the style of clothing was unformed in comparison to that of later centuries. Loose tunics or dresses with large squares of cloth draped as cloaks were the norm. The **costume** of Cymbeline, a sun to his subjects, was a worn and heavy old gold gown made of a silk-like fabric; the darkened hem was one expression of his clouded mind. Over this he wore a velvet cloak in muddied yellow and also partly darkened in uneven tones. This was cut asymmetrically and trimmed with rich embroidery. I chose to make the cloak asymmetrical to demonstrate that Cymbeline is psychologically unbalanced. The 'moon-like' queen only shines thanks to her husband's light that reflects on her; she was dressed in pale silver touched with black to make visible her evil intent. The dress was made of shiny silver satin; it fitted tightly and had a high neck. This was to show that she wished to prevent her feelings from interfering with her evil thoughts and intentions. A brittle and glass-like veil draped in angles indicated her fragile psychological state.

TWELFTH NIGHT

THE PLAY

The comedy deals with issues of identity and the confusion that ensues when individuals do not know themselves and therefore cannot recognize each other. Its mood turns sour when Sir Toby Belch, Maria and Feste mock Sir Andrew Aguecheek for his dullness. Then they ridicule and humiliate Olivia's steward, Malvolio, who is driven into painful isolation as a consequence of their malicious plot. Although in Shakespeare's canon this is the play that most wants to entertain, I found it frothy on the surface, but discovered a bitter profundity underneath. So I looked for colors, textures and styles that elaborated the outer appearance and disguised or hid what lay beneath.

Cymbeline

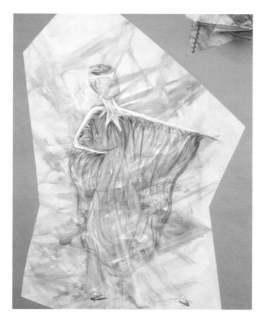

The Queen

THE DESIGN
Pastel Colors, Rich Textures, Fussy Styles

The flats used for the **set** were painted in varying greens to create a garden; bushes that were made from wire and cloth and painted in greens became places to hide. Curtains that could be drawn across different parts of the stage were used for the indoor scenes. To create bright, summery **lighting** I used primarily strip lights with blue and green filters to flood the stage, with several yellow spotlights directed at specific areas.

I found softer colors suitable for the ecstatic mood that *being in love with love* created and added frills, furbelows and other fussy details typical of the Rococo style to enhance the movement of the **costumes**. Both Sir Toby Belch, ringleader of the plot, and Maria, Olivia's maid, wore clashing oranges and pinks to highlight their comic nature, Sir Toby in the darker

and Maria in lighter tones, with added stripes. Sir Andrew Aguecheek's bilious green jacket and breeches were made in washed-out tones to express the weakness of his character. Malvolio, the vain and pompous steward wishing to appear humble, wore the black uniform of office, but made of elegant brocade. The straight velvet trimmings on his jacket stood out strongly against the garment's fullness and emphasized his mock-Puritanical attitudes. The contrasting elements in this design were used to expose the contradictions in his complex character. Feste, with the soul of a poet and somewhat distant from the other characters, wore a hip-length patchwork poncho with a hood, made of a variety of yellow tones to express his quick and lively wit. The poncho was lined with fine mid-blue cotton that was rarely in evidence. This was intended as a gentle pointer to a wisdom within him that he kept well hidden. The whole style of poncho and hood that enclosed his upper body wanted to express

how the world in which he found himself limited his movements and his initiatives.

THE TEMPEST

THE PLAY

In Shakespeare's last play, in which magic and enchantment feature as strongly as in *A Midsummer Night's Dream*, the human magus, Prospero, uses his
"so potent art..."
to direct a number of human destinies. His interventions also determine his daughter Miranda's future. Ariel, a spirit being of air and fire and Prospero's servant, yearns for the freedom that only Prospero can give him. Caliban, half-man half-beast, is a being of earth and water; just as Ariel he must serve Prospero until he can once again take possession of the island that had once been his own. Strong images

Sir Toby Belch

Maria

Sir Andrew Aguecheek

Malvolio   *Feste*

arose in me out of the themes of the powers of nature and of magic, and I spent time in woods and on the moors and heath observing clouds and the colors of different weather conditions. Then, one after another, I imagined myself as the different characters arriving on Prospero's island. I sensed their inner life and gave this expression in color, my primary design tool for this play.

THE DESIGN
Rainbow Colors, Varied Textures,
Mixed Styles

To depict the play's outdoor setting on an island, the **set** consisted of flats on either side of the stage painted in soft green and blue abstract forms, with a white cyclorama at the back. Prospero's and Miranda's dwelling, a cave, was built of chicken wire and textured papier-mache on a wooden frame and painted in deep purples. The general **lighting** effects were created with battens of floodlights hung above the front and middle of the stage and directly above the cyclorama. Floor lights lit its base. These were all fitted with filters in the three primary colors and yellow. Colored spotlights were used to highlight particular areas of the island.

The contrasting natures of the two servants, Ariel and Caliban, suggested the colors of their **costumes**: Ariel wore flowing pastel tones on light, semi-transparent veils; Caliban had the earth colors on small pieces of seaweed-shaped fabrics all over his large, amorphous poncho that completely covered his body. Each shape was as amorphous as the poncho itself, so that his movements, even though they were slow and heavy, constantly changed the shapes his costume created. To create a bulky shapelessness that bore little resemblance to the human form, a cushion was fixed at the back of the actor's neck under the poncho and gave the impression of a hump. To me Miranda represented the future; she was dressed in a silk shift in the soft blush rose of a spring dawn. Over this she wore a translucent cape in pale blue, creating a lavender tone in her movements, all as expression of the love for the King of Naples' son Ferdinand that was gradually awakening within her. Prospero's rough wool gown in a deeper blue contained both the blue of the ocean and the blue of the sky surrounding the island. For his cloak, one of the instruments of his magical powers, nothing less than the full color circle that occurs in the rainbow could be used with which to make visible that he was a true master of his *'charms.'*

Caliban: "Apart from the physical discomfort of the hump and the difficulty of trying to crawl on the floor while trying to show my face to the camera, this costume still did not allow for flowing or human movements. It made me clumsy and uncomfortable, but I felt sympathy for the character, as the costume gave me more a sense of an inherent disability than of a twisted psyche. I also discovered that there was still the possibility of a light touch and certain controlled gestures as my forearms, in particular, were entirely free, and my arms seemed central to what this character was able to do."   – Matt

Prospero's cloak

Ariel and Prospero

Caliban

X

DESIGNING A WHOLE PRODUCTION

PERICLES, PRINCE OF TYRE
AS AN EXAMPLE

"Therefore, my lord, go travel for a while,"

Pericles, Act I, scene 2

At the beginning of the creative process, I always ask myself how the designs of costume, set and lighting can best serve the spoken words and gestures of the actors and their characters. Having this question as a focus for the design has enabled me to find ways of melding the three elements of color, texture and style into a whole, so that the story of the play itself takes the focus of the production, and the details of costume, set and lighting are in second place. I could believe that I had actually begun to make this reality when my mother, with tears rolling down her cheeks, paid me a remarkable compliment: "The play was wonderful," she said at the end of one production, "but I am so sorry, I cannot remember a thing about your costumes."

This chapter sets out some of the insights important to me in coming to the design for a production of *Pericles, Prince of Tyre*. It also describes how I applied the principles already described to make the design a reality on stage, using simple and inexpensive means.

THE WHOLE PLAY

In *Pericles* Shakespeare takes his hero on a sequence of journeys to many places separated by the ocean; at the same time Pericles undergoes a sequence of inner transformations. These offer any designer a challenge, and my goal was to find ways to show how each of the six places to which Pericles travels can be distinguished from the others, and their individual moods highlighted and enhanced in all three aspects of the stage design. I also wanted to use changes in the costumes of the main character to express and make visible the stages of his transformation. I discovered during my readings of the play that Pericles and the ocean are the two constant elements running through the story, while the storyteller Gower links the strongly differing situations that Pericles encounters. I then noticed that each of these— and the characters within them—is in itself static and has a two-dimensional quality. Pericles' transformations on the other hand allow him to become a three-dimensional character.

THEMES OR MOTIFS IN *PERICLES*

1. THE HUMAN BIOGRAPHY

Starting by looking at *Pericles* as a whole, I discovered that one theme strongly present in the play is the archetypal biography of a human being, the phases of which I compared to the changing times of the day. The play opens with the idealism of Pericles' youth when he is moved to ask for the hand of Antiochus' daughter at the dawn of his adult life. Pericles is still young but has acquired some life experience; he celebrates his wedding to Thaisa in a mood of alertness and lightness at his midday of life. The play culminates in a mood of veneration, gratitude and fulfillment when, years later, a truly tested and mature Pericles rediscovers his wife Thaisa at the evening of his life.

2. THE STORMS OF LOSS

I noticed that three storms, both outer and inner, have a deep impact on Pericles as he travels. To me each brought about a different kind of loss: the loss of physical or worldly possessions, a loss that profoundly affect Pericles' personal feelings and loss of 'self' at an individual spiritual level. During a storm occurring between Tyre and Pentapolis Pericles' ship is lost, all his sailors drown and he is bereft *"of all his fortunes."*

When the second storm arises, Pericles is travelling from Pentapolis home to Tyre with his wife Thaisa. While at sea Thaisa gives birth to their daughter and then dies, depriving Pericles of his soul partner:

"O you gods!
Why do you make us love your goodly gifts,
And snatch them straight away?"

The third storm is within Pericles himself, of whom Gower says he

"... bears
A tempest which his mortal vessel tears"

as his ship lies at anchor in calm waters, and because of this inner storm, Pericles loses both his sense of direction and his purpose in life.

3. ASPECTS OF LOVE

Love is also a theme or motif that is present in many forms within the main and secondary characters. What struck me is that its negative aspects are found in the secondary characters while Pericles strives for its positive sides. **Lust** drives Antiochus to practice incest with his daughter in Antioch. **Envy** drives Dionyza to plan the murder of Pericles' daughter Marina in Tarsus. **Promiscuity** is the basis of the bawd's and her associates' life and work in the Mytilene brothel. Love of others or **altruism** motivates Pericles' gift of grain to the starving citizens of Tarsus. The **true love for an individual** is depicted in Pericles' undying love for Thaisa. **Love of the Divine** is demonstrated by both Pericles and Thaisa at Diana's temple at Ephesus.

PERICLES' INDIVIDUAL STATIONS

1. ANTIOCH

Pericles visits King Antiochus and his radiantly beautiful but nameless daughter, whom he wishes to wed. But to do so he learns that he must first solve a riddle, and if he cannot he will forfeit his life. After hearing the riddle he realizes that he is doomed one way or the other because he quickly guesses the answer: that the king and his daughter live in an incestuous relationship. So Pericles flees the corrupt and introverted world where

"Hell only danceth at so harsh a chime."

Dark & Heavy Colors, Rough & Smooth Textures, Asymmetrical Style

A black and deep red curtain was hung and draped as a backdrop at the back of an apron stage to create a heavy and dark **set**. The **lighting** consisted of a few harsh white spotlights illuminating specific playing areas. King Antio-chus' **costume** was made of heavy, black, smooth, synthetic fur, cut asymmetrically and embroidered with rough lumps of fabric scraps in a variety of reds, to create the impression of clotted blood. His daughter wore a tight-fitting, sleeveless dress of two layers of soft chiffon, red under black. The chiffon was draped horizontally and gathered on the left side of the body from neck to hem. It had a high collar that intended to indicate the character's constricted inner state.

Antiochus' Daughter: "I have seldom felt more promiscuous or on display than in this dress, despite its high neck. The cut is very tight at the waist, neck and thigh but loosens at the chest and hip which gave me the sensation of being rather exposed in those areas. Because it is snug at the leg, I was forced to take small steps and swing my hips more than I ordinarily would to keep my balance. The feelings of constraint and objectification elicited in modelling this costume were surprisingly strong. When I wore it I felt extremely attractive but also completely trapped." – Brigitte

Antioch

Antiochus: "The main feeling I got from this costume was dullness. The thick outer tunic was so monolithic it left me feeling inhuman and disconnected from any sensitivity to the world. The placement of the crown over my forehead again dulled my senses and made me feel closely connected to a base and unreflecting power. But the great slash in the tunic leaving one whole side of my body completely open made me feel extremely conscious of this weakness and awoke a need to disguise it with active malignancy in my actions." – Matt

Antiochus and his daughter

2. TYRE

Pericles flees to his own city but this, too, becomes a dangerous place for him. Antiochus' wrath pursues him across the seas to his own home in the form of Thaliard, who has taken on the task of silencing him. So Pericles resolves to
"go travel for a while …"
and soon boards ship again.

Cool Colors, Formal Textures, Grecian Style

The **set** for Tyre was a shallow stage with a blue curtain drawn across its entire width. The **lighting** was cool, created by using a pale primary blue wash with two straw-colored spotlights illuminating the actors. Pericles' **costume** was in the blue-green color of the sea, intended to highlight his loneliness on the one hand and his affinity with the elements around him on the other. Its slightly shiny yet elegant texture was cut in the style of a short, sleeveless, one-shouldered Grecian tunic; a longer cloak that

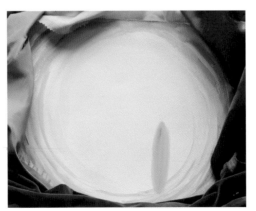

Tyre

hung from one shoulder complemented it. His youthful zest for life lived in both the texture and style of the costume.

3. TARSUS

Pericles' ship arrives at Tarsus, where both famine and its consequent misery abound and its inhabitants are compelled to
"Draw lots who first shall die to lengthen life."
Pericles brings relief by providing grain; for this generous deed he earns the gratitude of the Governor, Cleon, and his wife, Dionyza.

Natural Colors, Rigid & Flimsy Textures, Hard & Soft Styles

The **set** was built of flats at the sides of the stage and a white cyclorama at the back with a gauze hung in front of it, roughly painted in beige and brown tones. The flats were painted in pale, natural tones, the effect of which changed when they were lit with different colors. Otherwise the acting space was empty.

Tarsus

The **lighting** was a wash of mixed yellow and green that turned the flats and cyclorama green and made visible the renewed greening of the island. I did not use primary green because this would have turned the green surfaces in set and costume white. A similar mixture of yellows and greens was used in the **costumes** for the two main characters, Cleon and Dionyza. To accentuate Dionyza's hard, unfeeling character, she was dressed in a padded yet hard A-line dress hooped at the hem and made of many different greens. They were cut and then painted in sharp angles and appliquéd in clusters of patchwork. Her husband Cleon, the weaker of the two, wore a pale green, shapeless gown and cloak of soft fabric, which emphasized both his weakness and his inability to curb his wife's evil intentions.

Dionyza: "It was a challenge to wear this costume because I felt slightly off balance at all times. Because of the hooped hem, the skirt is hollow and swung dramatically when I walked, but the whole costume was still heavy and made of thick material, so I had the sense of becoming ever more fixed and plant-like. It is very difficult to describe how, but the costume awoke the sensation in me of having gone too far in one direction: I began to lose the sense of my humanity after several minutes in it." – Brigitte

Cleon: "This was by far the simplest costume I've worn, and I appreciated the cooling breeze after the density and discomfort of incestuous King Antiochus. But I definitely felt rather exposed, and as soon as I saw Brigitte as Dionyza I knew who was in charge in the relationship." – Matt

4. PENTAPOLIS

After losing his ship, all hands and his worldly wealth in a storm, Pericles himself is washed up on the shore of another city. There he finds himself in the midst of festivities that include a jousting tournament for the hand of Thaisa, daughter to King Simonides, whose sons
"sit, like stars about his throne,
And he the sun for them to reverence."

Pericles wins Thaisa's hand and they soon celebrate their wedding. This setting is full of joy, radiance and the true love that lives between Pericles and Thaisa, but then Pericles receives news that he must return to Tyre to reclaim his own throne.

Warm, Radiant Colors, Rich Textures, Formal Style

The **set** consisted of one heavy golden brocade curtain hung from the ceiling and behind a throne covered in red velvet that stood at the back of the stage on the left (stage right). The front was left free to accommodate the jousting. The **lighting** was bright and sunny; reds and yellows were used in a general wash. Floor lights and battens above lit the cyclorama in varying yellow and peach tones. King Simonides' **costume** was a warm yellow and gold gown and a richly encrusted brocade coat. Thaisa wore a shining satin sleeveless dress in pale peach with a chiffon overdress painted in rose, warm gold and yellow dyes. Pericles wore three successive

Dionyza and Cleon

Pentapolis

costumes when in Pentapolis: the first, a colorless, shapeless suit of rags in which he found himself after being shipwrecked; the second, his rusted armor that enabled him to win the tournament; the third, a royal blue gown and cloak made of velvet and brocade that he wore for his wedding.

Before the ship in which the couple is travelling reaches Tyre, a second storm arises, during which Thaisa dies in childbirth. Following the custom at sea, Pericles reluctantly casts his wife's coffin into the ocean. He then changes course for Tarsus to place his baby daughter, Marina, in Dionyza's care. From there he sets out once again for Tyre, where he grieves for his lost wife.

5. MITYLENE

Fourteen years pass; Marina has grown into a young girl of exceptional beauty and awakened Dionyza's envy. So a murderer is hired to kill Marina; however, she is kidnapped by pirates before the killing takes place and taken to the

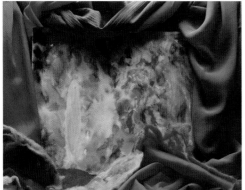

Mitylene

fifth setting, the town of Mitylene. There she is placed in a brothel where she is to work as a prostitute, but neither the bawd in charge nor any of her employees can corrupt her:

"If fires be hot, knives sharp, or waters deep,
Untied I still my virgin knot will keep."

Marina has the inner strength to improve both her immediate situation and the moral values of the brothel's clients. One of these, Lysimachus, governor of Mitylene, takes Marina to Pericles' ship in the belief that she can cure him of his unrelenting grief. Her stricken father soon recognizes her as the daughter he believed dead.

Warm & Cool Colors, Fluid Textures, Unstructured Style

A rough, Hessian curtain painted in dark reds and browns that was hung at the back of the left-hand area of the stage (stage right) created a simple **set**; a stool was the only piece of furniture. The **lighting** consisted of only footlights and spots in dim reds and greens that created a murky atmosphere. For the scene in which father and daughter are reconciled, only a couch was brought to the right side of the stage (stage left), and stretched across the whole width of the stage was the gauze curtain. A small area downstage was lit by soft, cool spotlights to transform the previously murky atmosphere. At the end of the scene, for Pericles' dream the lighting in front of the gauze was dimmed whilst behind the gauze the lights were raised to illumine the Temple Maidens at Ephesus. The bawd and her associates wore **costumes** in clashing orange and shocking pink. Their silky fabrics were draped in irregular

forms. In contrast, Marina wore a soft blue sleeveless muslin shift, while Lysimachus was dressed in a lavender tunic in a firm fabric. His deeper violet cloak, tinged with rose, was made of rich brocade. The grieving Pericles wore a deep blue, full-length gown in rough wool.

6. EPHESUS

The goddess Diana reveals to Pericles in a dream that he and his daughter must set sail for her temple in Ephesus to pay her homage. There he discovers Thaisa serving as a high priestess:

"… no more you gods! Your present kindness
Makes past miseries sport…"

A tender reconciliation takes place between father, mother and child.

Pastel Colors, Flowing Textures, Grecian Style

The **set** was a wide and open space, but to distinguish the inner sanctuary of the temple from its outside, the transparent gauze remained across the full width of the stage halfway

Ephesus

between the cyclorama and the front footlights. This was painted in a mixture of pastel shades using a sponging technique. The **lighting** for the cyclorama came from behind, using floor and ceiling battens with peach, rose and lavender filters. The area behind the gauze was lit by battens with filters in the same colors from the sides, above and below. Spots and floodlights were used to light the front half of the stage. When the action of the play was in the sanctuary, the front half of the stage was dimmed, so that the gauze became transparent. When the action took place outside the temple, the gauze became opaque, lit by lamps placed directly in front of it that stood in the wings. The **costumes** for Diana, Thaisa as the high priestess and the virgins had the pastel tones of rose, peach, primrose yellow, lavender and apple

green and were made of light silk. They were worn with transparent chiffon drapes in the classical Grecian style. Marina's and Lysimachus' costumes remained the same, while Pericles now wore a simple purple caftan.

7. THE OCEAN

The seventh space in which the story unfolds is the sea. Pericles encounters it in its extremes: when it is wild and stormy and when the waters are becalmed. Its ever-changing dynamic enables him to change, too. Only **lighting** was used to make this seventh space a presence on the stage. Before each scene began, the **set** was lit in a watery blue and green wash for some moments while the stage remained empty. The actors entered the stage only when the specific lighting for the coming scene had been brought up. Finally, when the action took place on board ship during the storm in which Thaisa dies in childbirth, the set consisted of a simple mast and sail held up by sailors, while the cast present on the stage swayed as if tossed by the waves.

THE COLOR JOURNEY IN SET AND COSTUME

My design for *Pericles* became a journey through the sequence of some of the colors of the rainbow for the settings, lighting and secondary characters' costumes, starting with the darkest, black, at Antioch, going on to using mainly blue at Tyre, green at Tarsus, yellow at Pentapolis, orange and pink at Mitylene and at the end the lightest, peach-rose at Ephesus. The constant color was the blue of Pericles' costumes. But to illustrate his metamorphoses, I took these on a 'journey' through the spectrum of blue. This began with turquoise (blue-green) and ended with purple (blue-red).

Ephesus temple

The Ocean

Gower, the Storyteller

XI

EXERCISES

"The head is not more native to the heart,

The hand more instrumental to the mouth,

Than is the throne of Denmark to thy father."

Hamlet, Prince of Denmark, Act I, scene 2

When preparing for a production of *Hamlet,* I was working with a group of ten people who had joined me to create the costumes, set and lighting. I was still devising the sequence of exercises described below and had gone through the stages for color and texture, when we arrived at the modelling for the set shapes. By this time the group knew the story well and they were capable of coming to entirely their own choices. The next goal was to elevate the floor level, and an animated discussion of the merits of the various options for the set shapes had just started. The main question they were addressing was where to place the available rostra. The passage in the play they found most relevant to their question was: *"What a piece of work is a man ..."*. They had grasped that Hamlet's striving for the truth of what it means to be human was a central theme, and to express this and the essence of Hamlet's own humanity, they chose the five-sided form of a pentagon. The group then created this pentagon as the central set piece by placing four separate rostra around the sides of the stage; its fifth side was the stage front.

These exercises are for those interested in researching and creating designs in a group, and their intention is to both awaken and free the group's artistic potential. When developing and using them over the last twenty years I have made a major discovery: The more the individuals are given opportunities to explore the principles of each element on their own, the more the group is able to arrive at a design for the production out of artistic principles and not out of personal choices.

COLOR EXERCISES FOR SET AND COSTUME

1. DISCOVERING THE CHARACTER OF INDIVIDUAL COLORS

Equipment: Crayons or paints; paintbrushes and water; paper; tables and chairs

Preparation: Ensure that all designers have their own set of colors in the same medium so that what they create is in that same medium. For the same reason give them the same size and weight of paper. Use a large enough working space so that everyone has enough space in which to explore on their own and not distract those around.

Exercise: Invite each designer to start with one color only, different from those chosen by the others, and then to cover the paper with the one color, using a variety of tonal levels, including the palest and the darkest.

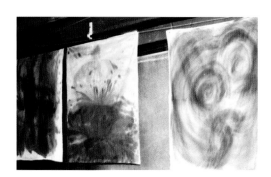

Request well in advance of this that everyone paint or draw freely, without resorting to imagery such as trees, houses or people. At the end ask the group to blend in a small quantity of any neighboring colors (in tonal sequence) to widen the color spectrum used. Draw their attention to the fact that the aim is not to overwhelm the main color with the neighboring ones. This exercise can also be done with dyes on cotton cloth.

Evaluation: Collect the examples and hang them on a wall in the sequence of the colors of the three rainbows, as described in chapter 2. Ask everyone to sit at a distance that ensures that each has an overview of all colors. Looking at one color at a time, invite the designers to share impressions, which may be single words, that express their experiences of the individual colors. Write the impressions in large writing beneath each color so that they can be referred to later.

2. CREATING A 'STRIP CARTOON'

Equipment/Preparation: After everyone has familiarized themselves thoroughly with the

play, prepare strips of paper, one for each designer, approximately six to eight inches high and at least a yard long, and fold them into three, four or five sections. The exact number depends on the number of climaxes or turning-points that the group has discovered the play to have.

Exercise: Set up work-tables so that the designers can sit with their backs to each other. Give one strip to each. Once everyone has both a strip and the same color medium, tell the story of the play. Pause at the three to five turning points of the play. During the pauses, invite everyone to use their colors to create the moods of the turning-points, but without using imagery such as trees, houses or people. Explain to each designer how to use the folded paper: From left to right, use one section for each of the turning-points, then fold the finished section under the rest of the strip so that it is no longer visible. Emphasize the importance of everyone's not only working individually but also of not referring to their previous picture or pictures.

Evaluation: Collect the strips and hang them on the wall beneath each other so that each scene becomes one column. Ask the group to sit at a distance and find and describe the contrasts and similarities in the separate sections. Invite each designer to share other perceptions; allow the sharing to lead to the discovery of which colors belong to which scenes. Encourage everyone to reflect on the colors that might belong to the various characters. Write the discoveries and reflections on sheets of paper in large writing so that they can be referred to later.

3. EXPLORING SCENE PAINTING TECHNIQUES

Equipment: Three, four or five (as many as there are sections in the 'strip cartoon') white flats and stage weights to hold the flats safely upright, or large sheets of white paper pinned to a wall; large quantities of plastic sheeting as underlay; broad decorators' paintbrushes; buckets of water thickened with sizing (or wallpaper paste); powder paints in as many colors as possible, including black and white; sponges; flat plastic or glass palette boards large enough to use as mixing boards; aprons (advisable)

Preparation: Lay plastic sheeting on the floor of the workspace. Paint three to five flats with white emulsion and leave to dry. Set up the flats in their vertical position and weight them, or pin sheets of paper to the surrounding walls. Mix the water and sizing as directed in the instructions until the mixture acquires a consistency that prevents it from dripping. Spoon small quantities of a range of powder paint colors onto the palettes and place these in front of the flats or sheets of paper. Place one bucket of paste and two or three paintbrushes alongside each palette in front of the flats or sheets of paper.

Exercise: This is a repetition of the sequence of steps used to create the 'strip cartoon,' using one flat for each section of the 'cartoon.' Seat the group at the back of the auditorium to create the maximum distance between the painting and the viewing. Suggest that two or three designers become the 'hands,' i.e., go on the stage and paint the first flat together. Invite the remaining designers to be the 'eyes,' i.e., to watch closely and suggest to the 'hands' how to proceed. While the group is painting and watching, encourage each individual to think about further developing the choices made in earlier exercises. Ensure that the 'hands' regularly become the 'eyes' and vice versa, so the collaboration among the individuals in the group can intensify.

Evaluation: Once the painting is finished and the tools cleared away, invite the participants to share their impressions of the effects. Allow the reflections to either confirm or adjust any choices made so far. Write the comments on large sheets of paper and hang them on the surrounding walls so that they can be referred to later.

Conclusion: Retain the flats so they can be used at a later date to discover the effect of colored lighting on the colors used on the flats or paper. Once the above study of the effects of the colored lights on the colored flats has been completed, the flats may be scrubbed clean with a broom and hose. They are then ready to be painted for the actual set.

TEXTURE EXERCISES FOR COSTUME & SOFT SCENERY

1. DISCOVERING THE QUALITY & CHARACTER OF INDIVIDUAL TEXTURES

Equipment: Pieces of fabric in a wide variety of textures

Preparation: At every opportunity beg, borrow or buy as wide a selection as possible of fabric textures and colors, from friends and family, second-hand shops and charity sales. Collect curtains, bedspreads and tablecloths rather than finished items of clothing or costumes; they provide inexpensive examples of unusual textures. Use a large enough working space so that everyone has enough space in which to explore on their own and not distract those around. Ensure that the floor of the work space is scrupulously clean.

Exercise: Spread the fabrics on the floor in a sequence of colors that freely relates to the color exercises. Invite the designers to walk around and between the fabrics in silence and to feel their textures and weights. Suggest that

everyone pick up the fabrics to observe how they move.

Evaluation: Ensure that everyone has an overview of the textures. Looking at one fabric at a time, invite each designer to share impressions, which may be single words, that express their experiences of the individual textures. Discuss what the suitable use of each fabric is within the production.

2. TEXTURES FOR THE CHARACTERS' COSTUMES

Equipment: Fabrics of different textures; pins; tape; tailor's dummies (optional); no scissors. It is advisable when exploring the textures to use the colors already chosen for the characters.

Preparation: As above for previous texture exercise.

Exercise: Spread the fabrics on the floor in a sequence of colors that relates to the color exercises. Suggest that the designers form

groups of three and in the group choose a character on whom they wish to focus. Invite each group to walk around and between the fabrics in silence, looking at them and feeling the fabric textures while they imagine the character.

Suggest that everyone pick up the fabrics and move them, observing how they move in relation to the character. Invite them to select two or three fabrics inspired by the character and take them to their individual working spaces. Either ask one member of the group to stand as the character or use a tailor's dummy. Request that the other two drape and pin the fabrics chosen onto the participant or dummy with the help of dressmaker's pins and tape, but no scissors. The aim is to create a three-dimensional sketch or draft of the costume. This same exercise can be explored with smaller models, for example, puppets, using silk squares or fabric scraps pinned around a stand.

Evaluation: Seat everyone at the back of the working space so that they can see the effect of the costume drafts from a distance. Invite them

to place the groups of characters alongside each other to observe whether the costume drafts work together. Then ask them to look at all the costume drafts individually. Encourage the designers to share their perceptions and insights so that the sharing leads to the discovery of which textures belong to which characters. Along the way make deliberate changes to some elements of the costume drafts, including 'bad' choices, so that the different qualities of the textures in combination with their colors become more apparent. Make notes of the discoveries and reflections on sheets of paper in large writing so that they can be referred to later. At the end unpin the costume drafts from the living models or dummies and re-pin them on coathangers so that they are available later for the lighting exercises.

3. TEXTURES FOR THE SOFT SCENERY

Equipment: Two rods or clothes rails with height extension pieces; two tables; three to five old chairs in different styles; fabrics of different textures; heavy-duty pins where available, otherwise dressmaker's pins; tape; no scissors

Preparation: The same as for previous texture exercises. Hang the rods or set up the clothes rails in such a way that they will be able to support the weight of lengths of fabric hung over them. Set out the chairs and tables in the working space.

Exercise: Spread the fabrics on the floor in a sequence of colors that relate to the color exercises. Ask the designers to walk around and

between the fabrics in silence, while they imagine the scene or scenes. Invite each group to feel and move the fabric textures while they imagine the scenes. Ask them to select textures for: background curtains, window hangings, sofas, chairs and tables. Divide the designers into two groups and suggest that they drape background curtains over one end of one of the rods or rails and test whether the texture can be pulled or draped to the side by lifting the fabric and tying it back with tape. Using the two ends of the second rod or rail, invite each group to hang lightweight fabrics, such as lace or net, over one end of the rail or rod, then to drape the heavier fabric or fabrics beside them, and then to tie them back with tape, as sample window hangings. Invite everyone to lay, stretch or pull fabrics selected for sofas and chairs over the chairs set. Using the tables, spread fabrics selected either as a decorative cover or as a tablecloth over them.

Evaluation: Seat everyone at the back of the work space to look at the effect of the various textures from a distance. Invite the designers to share their perceptions so that the sharing leads to the discovery of which textures can be used for which scenes or situations. Make notes of the discoveries and reflections on sheets of paper in large writing so that they can be referred to throughout the process. At the end store the draped rails or rods so that they are available later for lighting exercises.

FORM & STYLE EXERCISES FOR COSTUMES

Equipment: One table and chair for each designer; paper; leaded pencils; colored pencils, paints or any other color medium. It is advisable when exploring the forms to work with the colors already selected for costumes.

Preparation: Set up tables and chairs. Lay out paper and pencils/paints.

Exercise: Starting with a five-pointed star, ask everyone to explore human proportions in drawing as described in Chapter 4. Invite the designers to expand and contract the proportions of the five-pointed star and to explore how specific human characteristics can be expressed in the proportions of the lines. Then ask them to observe the qualities of the direction of the line (the vertical, horizontal and diagonal in both directions), first in the upper, then in the lower body and finally in the whole human form. Allow individuals to choose a character for which to design a costume. Using the discoveries made about the qualities of the line directions, encourage them to allow the form of the costume to emerge as they imagine the character. Once this has happened, suggest that they add the colors for the different parts of the character's costume from the choices made so far.

Evaluation: Collect the designs and then hang them up in character groups. Suggest that everyone sit at a distance to ensure that they have an overview of the designs. Then invite the designers to share the impressions of their experiences of: the whole ensemble, the groups of characters, individual characters. Write the impressions in large writing beneath each design so they can be referred to later. The costume designs are now the basis of the building of the costume.

FORM AND STYLE EXERCISES FOR THE SET

1. DISCOVERING THE STYLE IN MINIATURE FORMS

Equipment: One table and chair for each participant; clay modelling boards; clay (approx. one football-sized piece per board); cardboard boxes; knives. This exercise can be done singly or in groups of two or three.

Preparation: Set up tables, chairs, boards. Distribute clay and working tools.

Exercise: Using the clay supplied, invite the designers to create and mold a variety of shapes

in miniature. Then ask everyone to create models of: the physical spaces as they are at the turning points in the play used in the color and texture exercises, abstract forms that express the essence of the same turning points, e.g. tall, straight, short, curved, the forms of the objects (trees, rocks, furniture). Explore whether the forms belong at the back or the front of the stage. Remember that every shape casts a shadow or shadows.

Evaluation: Ask everyone to place the clay models on their modelling board as they might set them in the space for the production. Invite the whole group to sit where they have an overview of the designed shapes. Ask them to share impressions and experiences of: the spaces, the objects, the abstract forms. Write the impressions in large writing beside each design so that they can be referred to later. At the end cover the forms in plastic bags so that they remain moist; store them safely so that they are available later for lighting exercises.

2. LARGE FORMS

Equipment: Wooden poles 3 meters long

Preparation: Distribute one pole to each designer. Draw attention to the dangers of working with long poles: once a particular direction (i.e., vertical/horizontal/diagonal) has been adopted, it is important that everyone hold the pole pointing in the same direction until instructed otherwise.

Exercise 1 – Vertical Shapes: Ask everyone to stand in the workspace holding the pole vertically in front of them. Starting with either a circle or a straight line, invite the group to create a number of different shapes in the space (to build 'mobile walls'), holding the poles vertically in front of them. Repeat the same forms and shapes, holding the poles behind them. **Horizontal Shapes:** Ask participants to hold the poles horizontally in front of them. Starting with either a circle or a straight line, invite the group to create a number of different shapes in the space (to build 'mobile fences,' etc.), holding the poles horizontally in front of them. **Diagonal Shapes:** Ask everyone to hold the poles in a variety of diagonal positions. Starting with either a circle or a straight line, invite the group to create a number of different shapes in the space (to build 'mobile roofs,' etc.), holding the poles diagonally in front of them.

Exercise 2 – Ask the designers to create shapes with the poles both upstage and downstage. Invite them to create shapes with the poles on the left and right of the stage. Ask them to create shapes in the upper regions of the stage, near the lights, then in the lower regions, near the floor. Invite individuals in turn to stand within the created form and experience it from inside. Allow the same designer to observe the same form from the auditorium.

Evaluation: Invite everyone to share impressions of their experiences of creating the shapes. Pay attention to the variations in the experiences of standing in front of or behind the pole. Write the impressions in large writing so that they can be referred to later. Both the miniature and the large forms create the basis from which to design and build the set.

LIGHTING EXERCISES

1. DISCOVERING INDIVIDUAL COLORS IN LIGHTING

Equipment: A stage; white curtains or flats (sheets can be hung over colored flats); a variety of lamps (strip lights, spotlights, etc.); lighting control board; filters in blue, green, red and amber or yellow; two ladders

Preparation: Clear and clean the stage. Set up white flats or hang white curtains or sheets. If necessary cut colored filters to fit into the frames to be used. Check that the lighting control board is in working order. Fill the frames with the four colored filters mentioned above and fit the frames to the lamps. Suggest that between the individual phases of the exercises everyone rests or closes their eyes as often as possible. Be aware that the intensity of the colored lights can have strong and disturbing effects on individuals; pay special attention to everyone's well-being.

Exercise 1a: Invite everyone to move onto the darkened stage and crouch with closed eyes. Gradually bring up the blue strip lights. Ask everyone to open their eyes and begin to move as the color around them inspires them. Watch the movements closely, allowing the group itself to determine when everyone returns to their crouching position. Invite participants to return to their crouching position with closed eyes, gradually fading out the blue, so that the stage is again in darkness. Repeat this sequence with the other two primary lighting colors of green

and red, followed by the non-primary color yellow, ensuring that the stage is dark between the color experiences.

Exercise 1b: Repeat the above sequence, with one half of the group moving to the colors and the other half observing the movers. Repeat the above sequence with the second half moving and the first half observing.

Evaluation: Ask everyone to leave the stage and sit in a circle, if possible in daylight. Suggest that they share their experiences of the colors in lighting. Take note of how the individual colors have influenced those who have been moving. This influences the audience, too, mainly unconsciously. Write the impressions in large writing on sheets of paper so that they can be referred to later.

Exercise 2a: Allowing everyone to observe from the auditorium, repeat the above sequence for the same four colors as in exercise 1, but without returning to darkness between the colors.

Exercise 2b: Again allowing everyone to observe from the auditorium, repeat the same sequence as in exercise 1, this time changing, adding and combining the colors and building up the lighting levels until they are as intense as possible.

Evaluation: Ask everybody to sit in a circle, if possible in daylight. Suggest that they share additional impressions of their experiences of the colors in lighting. Write the impressions in large writing on sheets of paper for later reference.

Exercise 3: Invite everyone to stand with their backs to the colored strip lights and face the white flats. Gradually light the stage with first the blue strip lights and then the green ones. While raising and lowering the levels of the two colors, but without removing either color entirely, ask participants to gently move whilst observing the shadows on the white flats created by their movements. Repeat the same sequence, first bringing up the green and then the red strip lights. Repeat the same sequence again, first bringing up the blue and then the red strip lights. Repeat the same sequence for a third time, first bringing up the blue, then the green and then the red strip lights, again raising and lowering the levels of the three colors alternately. Finally, add yellow to the three colors and ask everyone to observe the effect. Repeat the same sequence, reversing the order in which the colors have been introduced. Follow this with an improvised sequence of colors.

Evaluation: Ask everyone to sit in a circle, if possible in daylight. Ask them to share impressions of their experiences of the colored shadows on the background. Write the impressions in large writing on large sheets of paper for later reference.

2. EFFECTS OF COLORED LIGHTING ON COLORED SURFACES & FORMS

Miniature Forms

Equipment: A space which can be blacked out; one clay modelling board per set of clay models as a miniature stage; the clay models made in the earlier exercise; four flashlights; miniature colored filters in the three primary colors and yellow; scissors and tape; white cloth or stiff paper or a board as a backdrop; table; chairs

Preparation: Place the modelling board on the table in front of the group. Create a miniature theatre space by hanging or creating at the back of the modelling board a vertical white backdrop out of paper, board or cloth. Set out chairs for the group. Cut small filters in the three primary colors and yellow and tape them to the flashlights.

Exercise: Once everybody is seated, invite one or more group members to set the forms for the first turning point in the play in the miniature stage space. Hand one flashlight each to four designers; invite the others to observe. Black out the space. Invite the four to experiment with distances, moving the flashlight close into and then away from the stage and lighting the stage with it: with angles, moving the flashlight high above the stage and then down to floor level and lighting the stage with it; and with the sides, moving the flashlight from stage left and from stage right and lighting the stage with it. Suggest that the others note the effects they have observed. Repeat the above sequence for the further turning points of the play.

Evaluation: Ask everyone to sit in a circle, if possible in daylight. Suggest that they share impressions of their experiences of the forms under the colored lights and the shadows the forms created on the white backdrop. Write the impressions in large writing on large sheets of paper for later reference.

Large Surfaces & Forms

Equipment: A stage; the three, four or five flats already painted in the exercises on set painting; three white flats; all the costume drafts created in earlier exercises; dummies or coat-hangers; artists' easels; a gauze curtain or scrim; lighting equipment as earlier; chairs

Preparation: Place the white flats on one side of the stage, the colored flats on the other and the set drapes in the center. Place the costumes that are still pinned to the dummies or coat-hangers in front of the white flats.

Exercise 1: Invite everyone to sit in front of the stage. Darken the auditorium. Light the stage first with blue strip lights alone, then with green alone, then with red alone, then with yellow alone. Repeat as required. Ask the group to observe the effects of the individual colors on the painted flats and on the costume drafts.

Then combine the colors, building up sequences, both prepared and freely improvised. Ask everyone to observe the effects of the different combinations of colors on the painted flats and costume drafts. Encourage them to take particular note of the effect of the red and green lights on the red and green surfaces.

Exercise 2: Using both strip lights and spotlights, change the source of the lighting. Light the stage from the front, from both right and left and from behind; light it from below and from above. Invite everybody to observe the effects of the different lighting sources.

Exercise 3: Using white spotlights only, light specific areas of the stage. Ask one or two designers to move in and out of the lit areas of the stage. Invite everyone to observe the effects of lighting the stage with white spotlights only.

Exercise 4: Hang a gauze curtain or scrim and repeat the above sequence of lighting exercises, lighting the gauze first from the front only, then from the back only and finally from one or both sides. Invite everyone to observe the effects of lighting the scrim from the three sources of light.

Evaluation: Ask everybody to sit in a circle, if possible in daylight. Suggest that they share impressions of their experiences of the colored lights coming from different sources. Write the impressions in large writing on large sheets of paper for later reference.

FINAL THOUGHTS

Anyone interested in design and who has gone through the sequence of exercises described in this chapter, discussed and reviewed the entire process, and used the notes taken in the evaluations of the exercises when necessary, should now be in a position to create the final design of the set, the costumes and the lighting with a good degree of confidence. As to the time they may take. These exercises need approximately forty hours, or one full week of work, if they are to be done effectively. They can be done either in one block before the production starts, or during the early phase of the rehearsals or run more slowly, parallel to most of the rehearsal process. Of course, the creative process does not end once the different components have been designed. It goes on throughout the building of the costumes and set and beyond that into the final stages of rehearsal and ultimately into performance. Only then can the designer begin to think that the work has come to some sort of completion.

XII

PRACTICAL ISSUES

"To show our simple skill,

That is the true beginning of our end."

A Midsummer Night's Dream, Act V, scene 1

When I was working in the wardrobe at Sadlers Wells, I was instructed to make a bellboy jacket for a ballet dancer. I had never made a garment for men, so I approached the task with care. Once I had been shown the various methods I was to employ and followed them to the letter, I was delighted that the jacket fitted perfectly when the dancer came for a fitting: It looked as if he had been poured into it. In fact, it fitted so snugly that it raised my boss's suspicions, and he asked the dancer to lift his arms as he would do if holding his partner in the air. As he did so, the seams ripped open and, slowly but surely, pieces of my carefully-sewn costume dropped to the floor. I was devastated at the sight, but realized that I had forgotten one of the instructions: Double-stitch every seam. This chapter deals with general practicalities and the specific crafting of costumes, set and lighting.

SCHEDULING

All aspects of backstage work conventionally take longer to finish than first imagined or planned. So scheduling backwards from opening night, make a plan of action that includes deadlines for the different phases of production, such as the completion of set and costumes. Before rehearsals start, schedule costume fittings, technical and dress rehearsals, allowing enough time for alterations before the first performance so that the inevitable problems can be resolved with as little stress as possible. Allow enough time for all the lighting rehearsals, bearing in mind that other rehearsals cannot take place on the stage at the same time. For rehearsals to build the lighting settings, ensure that there is a team on hand enthusiastic about changing sets and carrying costumes on and off stage and able to wait while choices for the settings and levels are made.

THE STAGE

One of the first challenges the designer may meet is how to organize and structure the stage and the surrounding backstage area. Assess the stage spaces carefully before embarking on the design, as the layout determines to what extent the design can be implemented. Where possible, use a playing space with a ceiling high enough to hang backdrops and lamps out of the audience's sight. Allocate enough space to the backstage area so that scene and costume changes can take place easily and actors can move freely from their exits to their new points of entry. Where possible, ensure that the backstage area also allows for scene and costume storage.

1. SCENE CHANGES

Keep set changes to a minimum. As necessary use or build lightweight furniture that can be easily carried on and off stage. Use heavy set pieces only when they can be on stage throughout the performance. If heavy pieces have to be moved, attach wheels beneath them that roll silently. On an uneven floor give the wheels regular attention so that they remain silent.

2. LIGHTING CHANGES

Ensure that the lighting technician can see the entire stage so that adjustments to the lighting plot can be made during the performance. Give the technician manual control of the lighting board, even if the lighting changes run automatically from a computer, so that adjustments can be made during the performance. Consider introducing any new lighting setting before actors enter the stage, given that the lighting creates the atmosphere or mood for the action that follows.

3. COSTUME CHANGES

Design the costumes with any necessary quick changes in mind. Determine from the characters' entrances and exits exactly where in the backstage area the changes can take place. Affix fastenings to the quick-change costumes that do not disturb the character's makeup and

hair. (Avoid zippers due to their unreliability.) Organize enough help for the dressing and undressing at the start and end of the performance, as well as for the quick changes.

SET & SCENERY

1. PLANNING

Know the play well and familiarize yourself with the director's vision or concept. Know the specific circumstances of the production, e.g., the number of rehearsal weeks, stage hands and technical and dress rehearsals. Ensure that set building and other technical requirements are incorporated into the overall rehearsal schedule. Remember that the simpler the solution, the more effective it usually is.

2. STAGE SPACE

Keep the acting and backstage areas as open as possible. Position exits and entrances with enough space for actors to enter and exit safely

and to wait backstage in full costume. Place the set pieces so that all backstage areas are concealed. Check sightlines from every corner of the auditorium. Avoid any refreshments brought into the backstage area for fear of accidents to set and costumes, especially when the space is dark during performance time.

3. SET MATERIALS

Wood: Use sturdy and lightweight timber; it has an infinite number of uses, so can be reused.

Avoid knots in timber; they are weaknesses in the wood. Avoid unseasoned wood; it can warp.

Metal: Iron is strong and rigid but heavy, whereas aluminum is light and easy to move but may bend. Chicken wire fixed to a wooden structure can be molded into any realistic shape or fantastic form.

Fabric: To make rocks and other forms for the set, soak canvas or calico in glue or sizing. Mold the fabric onto a chicken wire frame and allow to dry. Paint the form when it has hardened.

Paints: Use powder paints for scene painting; they wash off easily if set pieces are to be reused. Add wallpaper paste to the water to prevent the colors from running. Use sand, sawdust, gravel and matte, shiny or iridescent fabric scraps stiffened with sizing and partially mixed into the paint to add textures to painted surfaces. Apply paints with vertical and horizontal brush strokes to create a man-made impression, such as of houses and streets. Apply paints with diagonal brush strokes to create outdoor and nature scenes with trees.

4. SET ELEMENTS

Floor/Coverings: Ensure that the surface of the floor is even and smooth. If using a floor covering, take a material that absorbs the sound of footsteps, such as cloth or sheets of hardboard laid with the rough side facing up. Stretch any floor cover and secure it firmly along all edges.

Rostra/Ramps/Stairs: Build sturdy rostra, ramps and stairs and fix them securely into position. Ensure that any such pieces of set are available to actors in rehearsal as early as possible.

Walls/Windows/Doors: Build flats to be used for walls, windows and doors so that they can be opened, closed and slammed without wobbling the whole set.

Ceiling/Roof: When creating a stage roof or ceiling, avoid blocking overhead lighting and causing unwanted shadows.

Cyclorama: Be aware that a cyclorama restricts the number of entrances and exits.

Backdrops: Unless scene changes are part of the flow of the production, hang a backdrop that closes off the back of the stage during major scene changes so that the action can continue undisturbed at the front.

Flats: If flats will be used for more than one production, use a standard measurement of 2.5m x 1.5m that allows for multiple uses. To stabilize flats, build and attach to their backs wooden triangles of at least two thirds of the height of the flat, using hinges that allow them to lie flush against the flat when stored. Once in position, lay one or two stage weights or sandbags across the bottom strut. Paint flats either on the floor, with long-handled brushes, or upright and in their final position on the stage.

Fly Sheet: Hang fly sheets and backdrops from scaffolding pipes and suspend from pulleys attached to the ceiling.

Curtains: Sew a chain or lead weight into the curtain hems so that the curtains remain still whenever actors—either on or offstage—move close to them. Leave no gap between curtains and floor when hanging. Remove excess curtain fabric to avoid accidents.

Gauzes: Handle delicate gauzes with care; holes are easily created and immediately visible, especially when lit. Stretch gauzes by sewing hems at top and bottom and sliding a rod into them; this will prevent the strong shadows caused by creases when lit.

Furniture: Build basic pieces that can be easily individualized. Blend the pieces with the general character of the design.

Breaking Down: Breaking down is a process that gives décor a used look. This is necessary even when the set piece needs to look new, as the genuine newness of the fabric or other material can distract. Break down fabrics either before cutting or after they have been hung. To break down a set element made of fabric, spray it or splash it with dull paint or dye. Cut holes and fray edges with scissors, scouring pads and sandpaper to create a rustic effect. Spray a darker shade of the base color into the folds, to create the effect of curtains and furniture faded by the sun. Break down furniture and other set pieces with hammers, scissors and any other similar implements so that items appear used or lived in.

Shortcuts: When the budget is tight or there is no time to build new scenery, hose down and repaint any flats used previously. Use rostra of past productions in new combinations. Hang simple curtains to create an indoor setting. Hang greenery to create an outdoor setting.

LIGHTING

1. PLANNING & DESIGNING

Know in which areas of the stage the action will take place. Before building full-size scenery and costumes, build a scaled cardboard model of the set and install flashlights or small lamps as lighting instruments, attaching colored filters to the flashlights or small lamps where necessary. Experiment with colored light projected onto samples of both white and painted set surfaces and onto swatches of costume fabrics. Experiment with different miniature gobos before deciding on lighting textures. Experiment with how changes in the angles and sources of lighting instruments influence the appearance of scenery and costumes. Describe the moods that the design wants to create at the same time as using the lights on the model stage when presenting the lighting design to the director and producer.

2. PREPARING

Make an inventory of the permanent lighting fixtures and other moveable instruments available. Get to know on site the positions and effects of any lighting instruments already hung. If equipping a stage with filters for the first time, buy the primary and complementary colors and amber. Ensure that any standard gobos purchased are the correct size for the type or types of profile spotlight available for the production. An individual gobo can be made by cutting a square sheet of thin aluminum to size with a Stanley knife and with the aid of a paper or cardboard template to carve the design into the aluminum.

3. HANGING & FOCUSING

Hang the instruments so that they are invisible to the audience or directed away from the auditorium. Ensure when hanging and focusing that every area of the stage can be lit, with equal brightness as far as possible. Hang the instruments not only from the front and above but also at the sides and back of the stage and from below, behind a piece of scenery, for example, so that as many lighting options as possible are available. Hang footlights from the edge of the front of the stage rather than placing them on its surface, so that the audience can see the actors' feet. Hang the footlights at an angle that eliminates or reduces unnecessary shadows. Light the backstage area independently of the stage lighting, attaching blue filters to simple fittings to keep lighting levels low. When installing backstage lighting, ensure that it is not visible from the auditorium. Install color filters after the instruments have been hung and focused.

4. PLOTTING & BUILDING LIGHTING CHANGES

Using copies of a plan of the stage, with indications of where set pieces are positioned, make sketches of the areas in which characters move and stand. This will serve as a reference when creating the lighting plot. In a blank, single-sided copy of the script prepared in advance, use the empty space opposite the text to indicate: when the lighting changes take place, which instruments and color filters are used at each change and the level of light for each instrument. Ensure that enough time is available to build each lighting setting in a rehearsal or rehearsals arranged for this purpose. Use this rehearsal time to make adjustments to the position of instruments already hung. Rehearse the lighting changes on the lighting board until they flow smoothly.

COSTUMES

1. FABRICS

Avoid using brand-new fabric when possible; they can appear harsh under lighting. If using new fabrics, treat them with paints, appliqué and other techniques before using them for costumes. Where possible use plain fabrics; they offer greater freedom when decorating and choosing style, and patterns lose definition at a distance. When it is necessary to use patterned fabrics, paint them asymmetrically to enhance and strengthen the overall effect.

2. DYEING, PAINTING & APPLIQUÉ

Use natural fibers wherever possible; they take paints and dyes more easily than man-made fabrics. Test samples of fabrics to be dyed or painted before treating them. Start by bleaching the fabric irregularly to give an uneven appearance. Wash fabrics to remove the bleach, so that new colors added later hold. Add new colors by dyeing or painting the fabric. Uneven coloring conveys that the costume or décor has been lived in and imbues the overall color effects with depth and variety.

Fabric Dyes: After mixing the dye or dyes, use them as if they are watercolor paints. Spread the fabric out on a large flat surface, floor or garden lawn. Either splash, sponge, brush or apply the dyes or soak the cloth in dye and leave unstirred, so that the colors take unevenly. Wherever possible, use cold-water dyes, hot-water ones need large containers in which the fabrics are boiled, and this process may destroy the fabric texture.

Fabric Oil Paints: Spray or paint fabrics with oil paints specifically made for fabrics, as these allow fabrics to move after the paint has dried. Apply paint over the dye to further enhance the color. To avoid any rigidity in the patterning, make a cardboard template of the design and paint randomly through it onto the fabric.

Appliqué: To create an embroidered effect, sew fabric scraps onto the costume or scene panel. Paint over the fabric to enrich and harmonize the design. Add braiding and beading to heighten the effect of the appliqué.

Breaking Down: As with set pieces and fabrics, all costumes, even ones that need to look new, need to be broken down to give garments a used look. The fabric can be broken down at two moments: before cutting and after the costumes are completed. To break down a costume, spray it or splash it with paint or dye. Cut holes and fray edges with scissors and sandpaper to create a rustic effect. Spray a darker shade of the base color into the folds, to create hem and sweat marks. For crowds or groups, break down one costume with colors from its neighboring costumes so that they blend.

3. COSTUME BUILDING

Assessing the Cloth: The grain or weave of any cloth is made up of threads woven in two directions: those running lengthwise are the **warp**-threads, and those running width-wise the **weft**-threads. The warp-threads, the stronger of the two, are stretched on the loom; the weft-threads, woven across the warp, have greater elasticity and are therefore less able to hold the

shape of the garment or curtain. Examine the texture, the weave and direction of the grain to determine how to cut the cloth. Where possible build costumes on the straight grain from the shoulders downwards. When the warp and weft threads are of a similar weight and the garment needs to flow, cut the garment on the bias, using the weave of the fabric diagonally. To achieve a symmetrical garment that needs to flow softly, when the warp and weft threads are uneven in weight, cut the garment on the bias or diagonal with a center seam.

Shaping & Padding the Body: The body of characters such as Richard III, Sir John Falstaff and Sir Toby Belch may benefit from being altered through shaping and adding padding before the costume is cut, and this can be done in a number of ways.

a) Upper Body: Make a waistcoat comfortably fitted to the actor's body. Attach any of the humps and bumps of the character to this base, using layers of wadding made into shapes. Once the shaping is completed, cover the entire padded surface with a final layer of silky fabric so that the rest of the costume can move over it easily.

b) Lower Body/Crinolines & Bustles: Make ankle-length petticoats from calico, cutting panels wider at the bottom than at the waist. To prepare to fix the stiff steel or nylon hoops to the petticoat, sew at regular intervals horizontal bands of tape wider than the hoops themselves. Sew the tape to the petticoat at both the upper and lower edges, leaving an opening at each

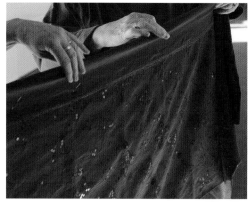

end of the tape so that the hoops can be inserted. Slide the hoops into the bands. Attach the bustle or crinoline to an undergarment like a short petticoat that fits firmly around the hips, to which the crinoline or bustle can be attached with tapes. Balance the two garments together to ensure that the main weight of the crinoline or bustle hangs at the back. Sew a frill around the petticoat hem just above the bottom hoop to ensure there is no ridge visible through the overdress or skirt.

CUTTING

Cut any costume cloth on a table, tailor's dummy or human body. Where possible, drape the fabric on a dummy or human body so that the cloth behaves as realistically as possible. To learn the skills required for cutting on the dummy or human body, practice with an old sheet or spare piece of cloth. Unless the design stipulates otherwise, cut fabrics using the warp-thread vertically, starting at the shoulder and working down the body. When working with delicate fabrics, cut a calico under-bodice and then build the fabric onto this base.

1. CUTTING ON THE BODY OR DUMMY

This technique requires courage, but once learned and practiced, it saves a lot of time because it keeps problems and fittings to a minimum. It is an organic, human-scale approach to costume-building and has the advantage of involving the actor in the creative process from the outset.

2. PREPARING

Have all the tools ready to hand: sharp scissors, a full pin cushion, ideally fixed to the wrist, plenty of tape and a piece of tailor's chalk or pencil. When cutting on a body, ask the actor to wear the undergarments that the costume requires, such as a T-shirt, corset or body padding. Fold the cloth in half along its length. Pin along the folded edge to make a center crease, so that the costume can be cut in two layers of fabric at the same time hanging on one side of the body. Select whether the costume's main opening will be at the center front or center back. (Side openings make for slower costume changes that can smudge makeup and disturb hair or wigs.) To create the opening at the center front or center back—the usual opening is at the back—measure a seam allowance of 2" (5cm) from the selvedge(s) of the fabric and draw a line with pencil for calico or tailor's chalk for other fabrics to mark the center. Use this unusually broad seam allowance to later fix the fastening to. Measure, cut and fit a length of tape around the

neck to carry the weight of the fabric while pinning. When the opening is at the back, align the folded edge of the fabric to the front of the body along the center line and pin into place on the tape at the neck and on the undergarments. When the opening is at the front, use the instructions below that apply to the front for the back.

3. CUTTING THE FRONT

When cutting on the body, leaving a seam allowance double the standard width means that alterations are still possible later. Experiment with how the fabric moves: Does it want to fall smoothly across to the shoulder or be draped loosely? Can the fabric be coaxed into obeying the demands of the style of the production? Pin the fabric into position along what will become the sewing line, starting at the base of the neck center front. Cut away excess fabric around one quarter of the neck, from center front to the position of the shoulder seam, allowing for a seam double the standard width. Smooth the fabric along and over the shoulder

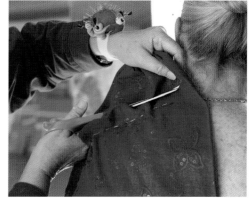

to where the sleeve will be attached. Mold the cloth down the body. Pin darts along the sewing line in places where the body shape and costume style require them. Cut away excess fabric in a curve from the shoulder down to the armpit, allowing for a seam double the standard width. Continue cutting away excess fabric down the side of the body, leaving a seam allowance double the standard width. If the costume has a seam at, above or below the waist, cut away excess fabric below this seam line, leaving a seam allowance double the standard

width. If the costume is to have no further fabric attached to it, or is a tunic or full-length garment that hangs freely from the shoulder to the knee or the floor, cut away excess fabric down the side of the body and then well below the hem level.

4. CUTTING THE BACK

Repeat the above stages, starting by aligning the marks for the opening down the center back and attaching the fabric at the neck center back.

Join the fabric along the shoulder to the front of the garment. Cut the sleeve hole. Pin the back fabric to the front fabric down along the side seam, allowing a seam double the standard width. Cut the hem length for the back at a length that corresponds with the front and the overall style of the costume.

5. CUTTING THE SLEEVES

Before unpinning the costume from the body, drape and pin the double fabric for the sleeve to

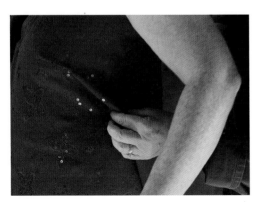

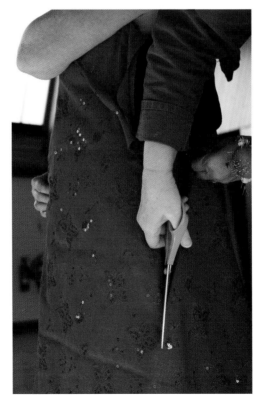

one shoulder, and arrange any folds or gathers as required. Cut away excess cloth. If the design does not allow the sleeve to be cut on the body, cut flat on a table.

SEWING & FITTING

Stage costumes should be durable and most audiences do not see them at close quarters, so the following practical tips can make the sewing faster and costumes more hard-wearing.

1. MARKING THE SEWING LINES

Remove the garment from the body, leaving the pins in place. Mark all the sewing lines either with pencil, tailor's chalk or thread, stitching the thread on the top layer of the fabric only. Make alignment or balance marks, again with pencil, chalk or thread, along the major seams. Remove all pins and lay the cut cloth flat on a table. Using pins, transfer the sewing lines and alignment or balance marks to the other half of the garment that lies below. Turn the garment over, mark all sewing lines again on the second half of the garment and remove the pins. Alternatively, sew through both layers with loose stitches, gently pull the two halves of the garment apart and cut the threads to leave little tufts marking the sewing lines.

2. BACKING

A costume backing, conventionally made of calico, gives delicate fabrics firmness and holds them in place. If calico is used to make a costume pattern, sewing lines can be marked and

corrections made with pencil. Cut the backing in calico, following the instructions above. Cut the outer cloth in exactly the same way, ensuring that the grain direction is identical. Tack the two fabrics together along the sewing lines and from this point on treat them as one.

3. LINING

Linings are made of satins and other soft fabrics and create a smooth inner surface for rough fabrics. The lining is cut and sewn independently, after the outer garment has been cut and fitted. They are best sewn into the garment by hand, because machine seams can alter the overall shape. Lay out the lining fabric on the table and use the pieces of costume already cut as a pattern. Before cutting, add an extra fold of fabric at the center back so that movement in the garment is easier. Transfer any adjustments to the lining after the garment has been fitted, adjusted and sewn. After sewing, place the 'wrong' sides of both garment and lining together, covering the rough edges of each. Pin together and sew into the garment by hand.

4. GENERAL SEWING & BUILDING

Sew the seams still to be fitted and altered with large tacking stitches on the machine. If the cloth is robust, they can later be pulled apart and resewn in smaller stitching. After fitting, double-stitch tight-fitting bodice and jacket seams. Sew seams on the machine as fast as possible so that they are as straight as possible. Once a seam is completed, trim away thread ends immediately. Avoid zippers because they stick at awkward moments. Use hooks and eyes instead, sewing them into the center back or front of the costume and giving them an underlay so that the wearer does not notice them. Test a corner of the fabric before ironing the whole garment. When ironing a heavy costume that pulls away from the board, either pin it to the ironing board with safety pins or place a table close enough to carry its weight. When ironing delicate fabrics, use a damp cloth. To prevent stains from excess moisture, wet one half of the cloth, squeeze it out, roll it into the dry half and squeeze again.

Fitting: Fittings are valuable for two reasons: They clarify what alterations are needed and give actors the opportunity to get to know their costumes. Request an exaggerated demonstration of the character's movements. Fit sleeves and other close-fitting parts of the costume so that the actors can move freely and comfortably.
Bodices & Jackets: Finish the open edges of the bodice (neck, hem, etc.) with bias binding. Use boning or stays on the calico undergarment to make a close-fitting and wrinkle-free bodice. Cover the stays or bone with protective tape and sew in by hand along the dart seams. When making a dress with a seam at the waist, sew the bodice and the skirt separately and then hand-stitch the bodice to the skirt at the sides.

Skirts & Trousers: To build a skirt or trousers with folds or gathers at the waist, make a stiff belt with buckram and attach the fabric. Before draping skirt fabrics over bustles and crinolines, sew tapes to the inside of the waistband at the sides and attach folds at different levels as required.

Gowns & Cloaks: To sew cloaks and gowns that have loose, full drapes, make a calico yoke and attach the cloak or gown to it, using hidden hand-stitches between the folds. To keep cloaks in place, fix tapes of approx. 1m length inside the garment at the top of the shoulders, bring them over the shoulders and under the arms to the middle of the back and tie together.

Hems: Keep costume hems at the front clear of the actor's feet to prevent tripping. Make hems longer at the back for dignified and elderly characters; they can slow the pace of walking.

Finishing: Finishing touches need to be generous, as details are difficult to see from the back of the auditorium. Mixing the above materials and techniques gives depth and richness to costumes under the lights. Use dyes and/or oil paints to heighten particular features. Add embroidery, ribbon, lace and/or beads and sequins as required. Finish the costumes with further use of oil paint where necessary.

Shortcuts: If building every costume in detail is not possible, focus on the central characters and indicate the supporting roles by alterations to second-hand costumes.

5. CLEANING & LAUNDERING

Give actors a fine jersey T-shirt to wear inside or underneath the costume, with sweat-pads for the physically active and those prone to perspire. Wash the T-shirts daily. Regularly wash cotton garments, such as shirts, blouses and tights, during the run of the production. Dry clean heavy and delicate garments when necessary and at the end of the run. Return only clean garments to the wardrobe at the end of the production.

MASKS & PUPPETS

1. MODELLING THE BASE OR MOLD

Masks are built on a base on a horizontal board, and **puppet heads** are modelled in the hand and then placed on a vertical rod. Model the base for a single mask or puppet head in clay or plasticine. (Clay works fast, is wet and cold and dries quickly if not covered; plasticine is firm, needs to be warmed before it is pliable and can be remodelled easily.) Keep clay or plasticine covered if it is to be reused. Make a template of the actor's face before modelling the base of a

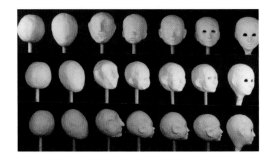

Seven stages of puppet head modelling

mask. Ensure that the eye holes or slits are in a position that enables the wearer to see and that the whole mask fits comfortably. Ensure that the profile is compatible with the image of the front of either a mask or a puppet head. To make several identical masks (for a chorus) or puppet heads (with different costumes), model a base out of plaster that makes frequent reuse possible.

2. PUPPET BODY MAKING

Face or Head Making: Faces and heads can be made from a variety of materials: Cloth or papier-mâché, rubber solutions, felt or carded sheep's wool soaked in PVA (polyvinyl acetate) and many other malleable substances that set firm when dry can be used to cover the base or mold. Cover the modelled base with cling film or petroleum jelly before applying any of the above materials. Decide how the mask is to be attached to the head, or the puppet head joined to the body, and incorporate this into the mask- or head-making.

Hand Making: Make hands from felt or papier-mâché. (Other substances, such as hard-setting clay, eventually crumble.) To give additional strength to the hand, build papier-mâché onto a glove for the masked actor's hand or a wire structure for a puppet's hands. To make the hand itself, sculpt felt soaked in PVA. Attach a wire loop or felt extension at the wrist to join the hand to the puppet's arm.

Puppets without Feet: Make the body of larger rod puppets with heads and hands from a costume of soft fabric that flows from the neck. Make the body of a hand-controlled puppet from a piece of fabric that conceals the hands. Drape the fabric over the hands and arms of the puppeteer or cut and sew it into a shape resembling a costume.

Puppets with Feet: Make the body from strips of leather or from pieces of wood hinged at the joints. Cover the wood or leather with padding so that the pieces resemble three-dimensional limbs. Attach a piece of lead to the hips to create a counter-balance to the head. Place a small weight in each shoe to facilitate walking. Cover the body with fabric in such a way that the puppet can move freely.

Painting: Painting a mask or a puppet's head is similar to applying makeup to an actor's face. Color masks and puppet heads with acrylic craft paints. Exaggerate the shading and highlighting so that this creates a balance to the stillness of the features.

Costume: Find the colors, textures and style in the same way as for an actor's costume. Choose fabrics that have enough weight to make the puppet's movements believable. Ensure that the costume does not control or limit the puppet's movements. Instead of changing a puppet's costume between appearances, make several identical puppets and dress them in their different costumes.

PROPS AND ACCESSORIES

1. ARMOR

Armor made as follows is light and comfortable to wear: Cut out a piece of heavy felt and make holes at those points where straps or ties will later be attached. Soak the felt in slightly diluted PVA glue and press into a mold. Cut away any excess fabric. Once the felt has dried and hardened, remove it from its mold and paint or spray it with metallic acrylic paint. Darken any dents or other uneven surfaces. Polish the armor with furniture polish to create a burnished look.

2. DECORATION

A small decoration can round off a prop, costume or piece of set; in excess, however, decoration can eliminate the object's definition and depth. Make a sample of any piece of decoration and test its effect under colored lights before making the full-scale article.

3. JEWELRY & MIRRORS

Caution is recommended when using jewelry or mirrors on stage because they frequently catch the light and blind the audience. Apply a small amount of grease to the surface of either a mirror or piece of jewelry; this will dull the glare without detracting from the overall effect of the prop.

FINAL THOUGHT

These chapters are intended, not as a fixed method, but to assist and enliven the imagination and offer possibilities of how to realize it into practicalities. They aim to engage the capacities of heart, head and hands of each participant to arrive at what best serves the whole. It is my hope that they will bring a measure of joy to this work such as I have been privileged to share with my students over the years.

INDEX OF CHARACTERS

"We are such stuff as dreams are made on;

and our little life is rounded with a sleep."

The Tempest, Act IV, scene 1

Ariel: *The Tempest*, a Spirit who serves Prospero in deeds of magic until he is released.

Autolycus: *The Winter's Tale*, a rogue and trickster.

Beatrice: *Much Ado about Nothing*, niece to the Governor of Messina, a fiery lady who scorns all men.

Benedick: *Much Ado about Nothing*, a young Lord of Padua who is minded to tame Beatrice and wed her.

Bottom: *A Midsummer Night's Dream*, a Weaver and one of the 'Mechanicals' who has an Ass's head placed upon his shoulders.

Caius Lucius: *Cymbeline*, general of the Roman Forces who has come to declare war on Britain.

Caliban: *The Tempest*, a savage and deformed slave, bound to serve Prospero.

Celia: *As You Like It*, Rosalind's cousin who chooses to be banished with Rosalind.

Cleon: *Pericles, Prince of Tyre*, governor of Tarsus, weak ruler unable to curb his wife's cruelty.

Clown: *The Winter's Tale*, a shepherd's son and simple country lad.

Cordelia: *King Lear*, third and youngest daughter to Lear who cares for her father in his greatest need.

Cymbeline: *Cymbeline*, King of Britain who has neglected his royal duties to Rome.

Dionyza: *Pericles, Prince of Tyre*, wife to Cleon and a jealous step-mother.

Dogberry: *Much Ado about Nothing*, a Constable who muddles the meanings of his words.

Edmund: *King Lear*, 'Bastard' son of Gloucester who plots mischief.

Feste: *Twelfth Night*, a clown and servant to Olivia who participates in ridiculing Malvolio.

Gertrude: *Hamlet, Prince of Denmark*, Queen of Denmark and mother to Hamlet who married the new king.

Gloucester: *King Lear*, a courtier allied to the king, whose eyes are cruelly gouged out by Lear's elder daughter.

Hamlet: *Hamlet, Prince of Denmark*, son to the murdered king and nephew to the new king.

Hermione: *The Winter's Tale*, Queen to Leontes who suffers banishment.

Jaques: *As You Like It*, Lord to the banished Duke, a melancholy spectator of unfolding events.

Jessica: *The Merchant of Venice*, daughter to Shylock and in love with a Christian.

King Antiochus & Daughter: *Pericles, Prince of Tyre*, an incestuous King of Antioch who tries to marry off his daughter to Pericles.

Lady Macbeth: *Macbeth*, who incites her husband to commit murder.

Launcelo Gobbo: *The Merchant of Venice*, a Clown, servant to Shylock who struggles with his conscience.

Lear: *King Lear*, King of Britain who misguidedly gives away his kingdom to his two eldest and false-hearted daughters.

Leontes: *The Winter's Tale*, King of Sicilia whose jealous nature causes great tragedy.

Lucio: *Measure for Measure*, a 'Fantastic' who busies himself with other people's affairs.

Macbeth: *Macbeth*, general of the King's Army who covets the crown.

Malvolio: *Twelfth Night*, steward to the lady of the house and victim of ridicule.

Mamillius: *The Winter's Tale*, young Prince of Sicilia who dies young.

Maria: *Twelfth Night*, maid to Olivia and co-conspirator to ridicule Malvolio.

Mariana: *Measure for Measure*, betrothed to the Lord Deputy and grieving at his faithlessness.

Marina: *Pericles, Prince of Tyre*, daughter to Pericles and Thaisa whose gentle purity is able to cure her father's depression.

Miranda: *The Tempest*, daughter to Prospero who grows up on the island to become a beautiful and truthful girl.

Oberon: *A Midsummer Night's Dream*, king of the Fairies who casts a spell on his queen and various mortals.

Old Shepherd: *The Winter's Tale*, who finds the baby princess and raises her.

Ophelia: *Hamlet, Prince of Denmark*, daughter to Polonius and in love with Hamlet, but is rejected and loses her mind.

Othello: *Othello, the Moor of Venice*, a noble Moor;,in the service of the Venetian State who is incited to mistrust his lady.

Paulina: *The Winter's Tale*, lady-in-waiting who cares for her queen.

Pericles: *Pericles, Prince of Tyre*, a Prince who travels to find a wife and meets with many adventures.

Polonius: *Hamlet, Prince of Denmark*, Lord Chamberlain, a pompous busybody whose advice leads to his own death.

Portia: *The Merchant of Venice*, a rich Heiress who disguises herself to preside in court as judge.

Prospero: *The Tempest*, the rightful Duke of Milan, banished by his wicked brother to a distant island.

Puck/Robin Goodfellow: *A Midsummer Night's Dream*, a Fairy and servant to Oberon, distributing a magic love potion to the mortals.

Rosalind: *As You Like It*, daughter to the banished Duke.

Shylock: *The Merchant of Venice*, a rich Jew who is wronged and demands a pound of his adversary's flesh.

Sir Andrew Aguecheek: *Twelfth Night*, a weak participant in ridiculing Malvolio.

Sir Toby Belch: *Twelfth Night*, uncle to the lady of the house who masterminds a cruel plot to ridicule Malvolio.

Stephano: *The Tempest*, a drunken butler.

The 'Mechanicals': *A Midsummer Night's Dream*, simple craftsmen who rehearse and enact a play in honor of Theseus' and Hippolyta's marriage.

The Queen: *Cymbeline*, wife to Cymbeline who drugs her king to further her own ends.

The Three Witches: *Macbeth*, foretellers of the doom that will befall Macbeth.

Theseus: *A Midsummer Night's Dream*, Duke of Athens, whose marriage to Hippolyta will be celebrated in four days time at new moon.

Titania: *A Midsummer Night's Dream*, queen of the Fairies who, under a spell, falls in love with an ass.

Vincentio: *Measure for Measure*, the Duke of Vienna who disguises himself in order to discover the truth about his people.

BIBLIOGRAPHY

"What do you read, my lord?"

"Words, words, words."

Hamlet, Prince of Denmark, Act II, scene 2

Bradfield, Nancy. *Historical Costumes of England*, London: George G. Harrap & Co., 1997.

Bruhn/Tilke, Wolfgang/Max. *A Pictorial History of Costume*, London: A. Zwemmer Ltd., 1941.

Craig, W.J. *The Complete Works of William Shakespeare*, London: Oxford University Press, 1905.

Gale, Elizabeth. *From Fibres to Fabric*, London: Mills & Boon /Allman & Son, 1971.

Goethe, Johann Wolfgang von. *Theory of Colours*, Bibliolife, LLC, USA, 2010.

Govier, Jaquie. *Create Your Own Stage Costumes*, London: A & C Black, 1900.

Harwood, A.C. *Shakespeare's Prophetic Mind*, London: Rudolf Steiner Press, 1964.

Hoggett, Cris. *Stage Crafts*, London: A & C Black, 2000.

Kleist, Heinrich von. *About Marionettes*, translated by Michael Lebeck, Mindelheim: Three Kings Press, 1970.

Laver, James. *Costume through the Ages*, London: Thames & Hudson, 1964.

Lloyd, Seton & Others. *World Architecture, An Illustrated History*, Paul Hamlyn Ltd., Reprint Society, Italy 1964.

Reid, Francis. *The Stage Lighting Handbook*, London: A & C Black, 2001.

Steiner, Rudolf. *The Arts and Their Mission*, New York: Anthroposophic Press, 1964.

_____. *Colour*, London: Rudolf Steiner Publishing Co., 1935.

_____. *Egyptian Myths and Mysteries*, New York: Anthroposophic Press, 1971.

_____. *Speech and Drama*, London: Anthroposophical Publishing Co., 1960.

_____. *Study of Man*, London: Rudolf Steiner Press, 1960.

Taymor, Julie. *Playing with Fire*, London: Harry N. Abrams, Inc., 2007.

Thomas, Terry. *Create Your Own Stage Sets*, London: A & C Black, 1985.

Wilsher, Toby. *The Mask Handbook, A Practical Guide*, New York: Routledge Taylor & Francis Group, 2006.

Acknowledgements

First and foremost I wish to acknowledge and pay tribute to the remarkable writing skills of my co-writer and editor Sarah Kane, quite especially for her commitment, tenacity and glorious bullying with this project. She has spent countless hours with me and with her computer and is responsible for my work's finding itself in print. Her pertinent questions and care to get the sentences to express what I really wished to say and say correctly I appreciate beyond measure, and for this I shall be always grateful.

Deep gratitude to Francis and Elizabeth Edmunds who, as my teachers, inspired me throughout my life, quite especially in offering me a deeper understanding of Shakespeare's plays.

Huge thanks to Dawn Langman for all she has taught me about directing a play and to John Watson for his brilliant lighting skills and tuition on lighting techniques. A special thank you to Heather Goodwin for the endless hours helping me talk things through, for the years of colleagueship and for an enduring friendship.

Warm thanks to Charlotte Fischer for her artistry in photography and to Magdalena Gadaj for her talented graphic design of the book sample. Many thanks for costume modelling charm and pertinent comments by Brigitte Allgood, Lara Gardner and Matt Blissett.

Thank you to my publisher, David Mitchell of AWSNA Publications, who has believed in my work and offered me friendship over many years.

My thanks also to many friends, colleagues and students who have supported me in my work, both in conversation and with generous financial donations, without which I could not have achieved this book. Their interest and enthusiasm have been important to me and wonderful.

Lastly, to my husband Michael Spence, a thank you far beyond what those words can say, for his belief in me and in my commitment to the arts and crafts and for his uncomplaining patience with my computer questions and endless struggles with this project.